Indian Summer
Notebook

Collected writings of Henry Williamson previously published by
The Henry Williamson Society

Contributions to the Weekly Dispatch, 1920-21
Days of Wonder
From a Country Hilltop
Genius of Friendship: T E Lawrence
A Breath of Country Air, Parts I and II
Spring Days in Devon
Pen and Plough
Threnos for T E Lawrence
Green Fields and Pavements
The Notebook of a Nature-lover

In memory of
Brocard Sewell, O. Carm.
1912-2000

Priest, printer, writer
and editor of
The Aylesford Review

Vice-President of
The Henry Williamson Society

Indian Summer Notebook

A Writer's Miscellany

BY

Henry Williamson

WITH AN ESSAY BY
Brocard Sewell, O. Carm.

THE HENRY WILLIAMSON SOCIETY

This collection first published 2001

The Henry Williamson Society
14 Nether Grove
Longstanton
Cambs

Text © The Henry Williamson Literary Estate 2001
'Henry Williamson' by Fr Brocard Sewell © British Province of the
Carmelite Order 2001
Illustration © Michael Loates 2001

Standard edition ISBN 1 873507 18 6
Limited edition ISBN 1 873507 19 4

All rights reserved. No part of this publication may be
reproduced, stored in a retrieval system, or transmitted, in any
form or by any means, electronic, mechanical, photocopying,
recording or otherwise, without the prior permission of the
copyright owners

Typeset by John Gregory
Printed and bound in Great Britain

INDIAN SUMMER NOTEBOOK

CONTENTS:

	Page
Editor's Note and Acknowledgements	vii
Henry Williamson, by Fr Brocard Sewell	3
Out of the Prisoning Tower	8
The Christmas Truce	13
When I Was Demobilised	24
Richard Jefferies	28
A First Adventure with Francis Thompson	40
English Farming	53
The Winter of 1941	57
Indian Summer Notebook	73

Editor's Note and Acknowledgements

This present selection of Henry Williamson's work comes from a number of sources. It consists of little-known introductions to books; contributions to anthologies and magazines; a series of articles in the *Evening Standard*, and a significant essay in the edition of Francis Thompson's *The Mistress of Vision* issued by Saint Albert's Press, whose publisher was Fr Brocard Sewell.

If the selection has a theme, it is one of people, places and events that had a far-reaching effect on Henry's life – his schooldays, the Christmas Truce on the Western Front in 1914, the writer Richard Jefferies and the poet Francis Thompson, his Norfolk farm and, of course, North Devon.

The Henry Williamson Society dedicates this book to the memory of Fr Brocard Sewell, who died on April 2, 2000. Fr Brocard had a very high regard for Henry, both as a friend and as an important author. In the post-World War II years he championed Henry's writing, and in particular the early volumes of *A Chronicle of Ancient Sunlight*, in the literary magazine that he founded and edited, *The Aylesford Review*, one issue of which was devoted solely to Henry. When the Society was founded in 1980, three years after Henry's death, he became a Vice-President, and at its first meeting gave a memorable paper on 'Henry Williamson: Old Soldier', with readings by the late Frances Horowitz.

In tribute to Fr Brocard, we include as a preface his article 'Henry Williamson', which was first printed in *John O'London's Weekly* in 1961. It is reprinted now by permission of the British Province of the Carmelite Order.

The Henry Williamson Society gratefully acknowledges the permission of the Trustees of the Henry Williamson Literary Estate to publish this collection.

John Gregory

Henry Williamson

by

BROCARD SEWELL, O. CARM

Henry Williamson's first book, *The Beautiful Years*, was published 40 years ago, in 1921. Over this long period, he has maintained a steady and prolific output of novels, nature writings, essays, and works of autobiography. *The Beautiful Years*, a novel of childhood, was begun during the last year of the Great War, through the whole of which the young author had served on the battlefields of France and Flanders. It was well reviewed, and sold 520 copies. Its sequel *Dandelion Days* (1922) was less well received and was soon remaindered. In its later, revised edition *Dandelion Days* is a serious, yet immensely entertaining, story of boyhood and schooldays. The truth and humour of the classroom scenes are balanced by passages which presage Williamson's later fame as a nature writer.

The story of Willie Maddison, the hero of these early novels, is completed in *The Dream of Fair Women* and *The Pathway* (1928). The narrative, reflecting in part the author's own experiences, now takes on a graver note. *The Dream of Fair Women* describes Maddison's rootless life after the demobilisation of 1918 and his disillusionment with the post-war world. *The Pathway*, a story of unhappy love ending with the hero's tragic death by drowning, reveals Williamson's gifts as an observer and interpreter of West Country life and character, to be developed later in his *Tales of a Devon Village*.

The Pathway, which closes the series of four novels known collectively as *The Flax of Dream*, was immediately recognised as the work of a potentially great writer, and was praised by John Middleton Murry and Edward Garnett for its truthfulness and sensibility.

The Flax of Dream was a subjective or romantic treatment of the theme of redemption. Its underlying motif derives in part from a central event in the life of the writer. References to this experience abound in Williamson's works, but the fullest description, of which we can quote only an extract, occurs in his later book *The Story of a Norfolk Farm* (1939):

INDIAN SUMMER NOTEBOOK

On Christmas Eve of 1914 we were in the support line, about two hundred yards inside Plugstreet Wood. It was freezing. Our overcoats were stiff as boards, our boots were too hard to remove, but we rejoiced. The mud was hard too! Also, happy thought, we would be able to *sleep* that night. Then came a message from brigade headquarters. Wiring parties were required in no man's land all night. And there would be a moon. We would have to work only fifty yards from the German machine-guns in the White House opposite the eastern edge of the wood . . .
  For an hour we worked in silence, in a mysterious soundlessness. What had happened? We began to talk naturally as we drove in stakes and pulled out concertinas of prepared wire. There was no rifle-firing either up or down the line . . . At midnight we were laughing as we worked. We heard singing from the German lines – carols the tunes of which we knew. I noticed a very bright light on a tall pole, raised in their lines. Down opposite the East Lancs trench, in front of the convent, a Christmas tree, with lighted candles, was set on their parapet. The unreal moonlight life went on, happily. Cries of 'Come over, Tommy! We won't fire at you!'
  A dark figure approached me, hesitatingly. A trap? I walked towards it, with bumping heart. 'Merry Christmas, English friend!' We shook hands, tremulously. Then I saw that the light on the pole was the Morning Star, the Star in the East. It was Christmas Morning.

After the war of 1914-18 Henry Williamson obtained a post in Fleet Street on *The Evening News*. In the offices of that paper he met Arthur Machen, who was employed as the paper's star reporter. Machen's books, *The Hill of Dreams* and other works of near-genius, were not widely read, and their author regarded his career as a journalist as a kind of slavery. Out of the bitterness of his own experience Machen strongly advised Williamson not to try to be a writer, but to 'go and keep pigs'.
  In Fleet Street, Williamson, whose hobby as a boy had been natural history, soon began to make a reputation for himself by his articles on wild life, some of which were later collected in his books *The Lone Swallows* and *The Peregrine's Saga*.
  In 1928, the year of *The Pathway*, came his first great success with the publication of *Tarka the Otter*. This was at once recognised as a great piece of nature writing, in the tradition of Richard Jefferies and W.H. Hudson but with its own note of originality. *Tarka* was awarded the Hawthornden Prize and was acclaimed as a masterpiece by John Galsworthy.

HENRY WILLIAMSON

After his early Fleet Street days, Williamson had left London and settled in a tiny cottage in North Devon. There he acquired a strange family of cats, dogs, gulls, buzzards and magpies: and also a tame otter cub. After being caught in a trap the otter cub was lost. Afterwards, when out with the Hunt, Williamson always dreaded seeing his own otter killed; and so, as Elinor Graham says in her introduction to the Puffin edition of *Tarka*, 'he entered the otter's world for a time and it became more real to him than the world of men.'

Tarka was followed, in 1935, by *Salar the Salmon*, available today, with Tunnicliffe's illustrations, in Faber's paperbacked editions. This book, put off month after month, proved an agony to write but was eventually completed quickly. 'The style,' the author says, 'is that of one self-compelled to complete a work before the subject could be seen in detachment, one result of being confined to a narrow valley for several years, and dominated by ambition to bring the sight of water, tree, fish, sky, and other life upon paper.' *Salar* has proved scarcely less popular than *Tarka*.

With the general public it is on *Salar* and *Tarka* that Williamson's fame chiefly rests. The public like an author to stick on the whole to one vein of work, so that Henry Williamson is usually thought of as a nature writer who has written some novels as a sideline. This is an ill-balanced concept which reminds one of how Baron von Hügel, when acclaimed by *The Times* as 'the greatest living apologist for the Roman Church', replied that having hoped to do well in the dog class he was much discouraged at being first prize among cats! Henry Williamson, understandably, feels much the same when he is asked: 'Why don't you write something else like *Tarka*?'

It had always been Williamson's intention to follow *The Flax of Dream* with the story of Willie Maddison's London cousin Phillip, who appears here and there in the book. This complementary series of novels was intended to present the same underlying theme, but to be written on the classic or objective pattern. 'Twenty years were to pass before the first sentence of the new series of novels was written. And during those twenty years the proverb of William Blake was chronically before my mind: "He who desires but acts not breeds pestilence".'

At last, in 1951, Macdonald and Company published *The Dark Lantern*, the first volume of *A Chronicle of Ancient Sunlight*, which will probably comprise thirteen books in all. Eight have appeared so far;

the ninth, *The Innocent Moon*, is ready for publication, the tenth nearly so.

The Dark Lantern recreates in loving detail the lost world of late Victorian London suburbia and mercantile materialism, and describes the courtship of Richard Maddison and Hetty Turney, ending with the birth of their little boy Phillip. *Donkey Boy* and *Young Phillip Maddison* are the story of Phillip's schooldays; with *How Dear Is Life* we reach the last summer of the pre-1914 world. *A Fox Under My Cloak*, *The Golden Virgin*, and *Love and the Loveless* are the record of Phillip's soldiering life: at Loos, the Somme, and Passchendaele. In *A Test To Destruction* (1960), Phillip is with the Fifth Army in France during the terrible battles of 1918, after which we leave him, demobilised, about to try to earn his living in Fleet Street. The whole series is planned to end on the eve of the war of 1939-1945.

So far the saga has made its way slowly; but among critics who have recognised its rare merits are outstanding names such as those of Middleton Murry and George D. Painter. There are signs that the tide is turning. With the publication of *A Test To Destruction* last autumn many of the reviews took on a new tone, and readers were given, for the first time, some idea of the scale and importance of the work on which Williamson is now engaged.

'What, I am asked,' says Henry Williamson in *Some Notes on The Flax of Dream*, 'is the basic feeling, or faith, of my authorship? . . . Shall I confess what I believe deeply within myself? That life is a Spirit; that the artist is but a medium of the Spirit of life.'

Henry Williamson is not usually thought of as a religious writer; but such, in the truest sense of the word, I believe him to be. He is a man who has lived from Christmas Eve 1914 until today haunted by the darkness of men's minds, yet knowing that light shines in the darkness, and that the darkness cannot extinguish it. In saluting this 'giant writer', as Maurice Wiggin has recently styled him, on the fortieth anniversary of the publication of his first book, I feel I cannot do better than to quote from the concluding paragraphs of his Wedmore Memorial Lecture of 1959 on *Some Nature Writers and Civilisation*:

> It seemed to me that now the age of so-called 'idleness', or leisure to relax, was a possibility: and that possibility was in part due to wars after which, despite all, the slums had begun to die. And that the 'near-madness' of

the fully-articulate of one age can sometimes be sanity and clear-sightedness of the next.

But we must not condemn those who do not see so quickly as the visionaries, for it is only a question of time: and in the words of Richard Jefferies, 'Now is eternity; now is the immortal life'.

John O'London's Weekly
21 September 1961

Out of the Prisoning Tower

Nearly all of my generation in Britain when young lived under a fairly strict Victorian discipline. Generally speaking, discipline was imposed at an early age in the nursery, and continued more or less rigidly – the cane alone being pliable – through one's schooldays. Not all children lived with the spirit of fear, however; but it is mainly true to say that many a small boy suffered malformation of the spirit in the first place through chronic fear in his father's home.

If on the other hand there was love within the home, both parents being in balance together, that and not fear was the base on which the child formed its existence, and its future living.

A child lacking love forms itself alone. It will live mainly in a world of fantasy. Francis Thompson, writing his essay on Shelley in the Nineties, startled many good people with his revelations of what the child was, something which felt more keenly than even adults. 'Thus beset, the child fled into the tower of his own soul, and raised the drawbridge.' Had Thompson been born a generation later, he might have added the epithet *loveless* before 'child'; and that sometimes the loveless child rushes wildly out of its prisoning tower, to steal (fortifying itself with possessions); to release tensions by setting fire to dry grassy fields; to arm itself with a horse-pistol costing ninepence in a junk shop, to load it with black powder and rammed newspaper wads, thus to advertise, amidst wonderful blue smoke, its own importance; to cherish under his Norfolk jacket a white rat which he loved more than any member of his family; and to suffer paternal canings which, on the naked flesh, raised weals, as seen in the looking glass of the bedroom, lasting up to ten days.

Thus, in all classes – and a repressive discipline was often the more severe as family property was the more extensive – was 'character' or eccentricity formed, often to produce results in later life 'due to sturdy individuality'. Men are animal at base, and animals are essentially fine creatures in the wild, unlike the half-tamed creatures of early nomadic tribes, whose literature speaks of them with fear, contempt, and warning, for that they were scavengers, often of the dead, and as such barred as food. The pig, for example.

School was an extension of my 'wild boy' (my father's words) fears (my words). But I was not always afraid. Looking back over nearly fifty years to my boyhood, I realise how fears were often evaded, if their effects are not entirely lost in the elderly man today.

I attended what was originally described as 'the Free Grammar School in the Borough', established 'of all the best orders and exercises in use at the Free Schooles at Westminster, Paul's and Merchant Taylors' School, and in the Public Free School at Eaton'.

The school was at Blackheath. Its founder, in the days of his youth before he created the school partly as an act of penance about 230 years before I arrived there, had badly blotted his copybook by making a speech in favour of the beheaded Earl of Essex, in the hall of Christ Church at Oxford. The speech was reported as sedition to the Lord High Treasurer of England and, his arms bound with cords, the undergraduate was taken to Newgate. But the Lord High Treasurer advised the Queen to show mercy to the youth, who, in his later age, as a priest of the parish of Loos'm, as it was still called when I was a boy, devoted himself to good works and the re-establishment of a Free School.

The masters of this establishment, when in due course my nervous self attended there, in a cousin's reach-me-down Eton jacket and trousers and hobnailed boots, with one exception, were amiable and kind. Among the bigger boys of Lower School there were bullies, who occasionally hunted and sat on me in one or another of the dark lobbies, during the luncheon hour. They held my head underwater while I was learning the breaststroke in the Ladywell Baths, the reason being, I think, that the small thin child with the abnormally large brown eyes gave out an irritating timidity and inability to be as other boys. These roughs, as I thought of them, were escaped from by climbing up a chimney between two buttresses supporting the southern walls of class-rooms abutting on the playground. By pressing with plimsolled feet and shoulders alternately, one could get to the top, trembling and suppressing cries, and claw oneself up to an acre or so of roofs and chimney stacks high above the ordinary world.

A sack stuffed into the chimneypot of the Head Master's study caused some bother one winter; the culprit confessed the instant he saw that his crime was discovered, and received five strokes of the cane, while with eyes shut (as ordered) he was stretched over a chair in order that, as far as was possible, the insulating effect of loose cloth be eliminated.

Canings had an invariable ritual, or dogma, on such occasions. The Head Master was gentleness itself, during this preparatory phase. 'Close your eyes; and think.' Pause. 'I have misbehaved.' Pause. 'It shall not happen again.' Pause. A smut floated down upon one extended hand. *Wallop.* 'Think!' Pause. 'It shall not happen again.' *Wallop.* 'Think! Quite still.' *Wallop.* 'An extra one for wriggling, sir. Think now. "I must get that mental power! I must not waste the time of others like this again."' *Wallop.* 'You wriggled again, sir! Quite still, now. Think! "I must raise my standard of honour."' *Wallop.*

I had the whack about a dozen times a year, on average, when I was a member of the Upper School. As an insurance against pain, part of an old leather satchel was sewn to the inside seat of my knickerbockers. Did the *wallops* resound somewhat alarmingly loud? My tears flowed the more abundantly, my face expressed despairing contrition, the less the stings failed to penetrate my shield. At sixteen years, to my shame, I still had a small body, treble voice, and staring brown eyeballs, not blue like all proper boys, as my father told me at three years of age. His eyes were blue, like the Head Master's, mine took after my mother's, which easily filled with tears like my own, to my father's exasperation and complaint.

What did I learn there, beyond the need to be shifty, two-faced, and the realisation that I was the 'worst boy in the school', as so often one heard while staring at the carpet in the Head Master's study? In the Upper Fifth we were taken by the Head himself, for Latin, Euclid, Trigonometry, and High Mathematics (or the foothills thereof, by way of the Binomial Theorem, Differential Calculus, and Projectiles – which very soon afterwards some of us were to experience in practice). I confess that these subjects were, without exception, mysteries to me. On the margins of Ovid's *Metamorphoses*, and other incomprehensible volumes, I made pencil notes of birds and their eggs, trees, fish, and animals around the lakes and trees of the Dowager Countess of Derby's park and lands at Keston, where I had permission to roam and where I freed myself of all home and school thoughts. Thither I biked on Wednesday and Saturday afternoons on my £4 19s. 6d. three-speed Swift, over the new roads of jarrah-wood blocks in which the rails of electric trams were embedded. Pheasants, hares, plover, pigeons could still be seen in the fields a mile or so from the school; trout idled in the upper reaches of the Ravensbourne, although the roach, rudd, and willows of its tributary Quaggy were gone, the brook running smooth and unwimpling in a concrete bed under a pavement before new tall shops in the High Street. I felt this change mournfully, for the spirit of wild life was now dominant in my secret living.

In winter, fogs of deep yellow often made dark the midday and it was cold. The windows of the Sixth Form were invariably closed, where thirty-two boys sat in pairs at sixteen varnished desks, grooved with many a knife, pencil, and pen recording initials and devices, while unending thoughts moved without will through heads avoiding the keen blue eyes and pink dome of wisdom, truth and honour everlastingly striving to uplift dull nature to the peaks. The classroom had for me a distressing smell, with hot air arising from pipes under gratings. Ceaselessly the Head, a brilliant scholar named F.W. Lucas, urged us to work harder, to get that mental power, illustrated by clenched fist vibrated like a metronome across his own brows. In his young manhood this exceptionally gifted man had obtained first place in the honours list for English History, Language and Literature at London University, together with first place for his M.A. Degree in Logic, Philosophy, and Economics; he had also taken a research course in Psychology for his Ph.D. at Freiburg, under Professor Munsterberg.

'Hard at it, boys, hard at it! Get that mental power! I saw your eyes, Williamson! Foxy, sir, foxy! No sugar in your tea for a week? Agreed? Very well. Now concentrate. Quite quiet, boys, quite quiet!' He would leave the room for a few minutes. Immediately the silence would erupt into gusty relief. 'Open the window, for God's sake. I'm stifling!' One unheeded cry among a buzz of voices. Perhaps the study door behind us would open suddenly, catching a figure pointing at the moisture running down the windows.

'Come along, sir! I'll gi'e you that cane! You will have to leave this school, sir, if you are not careful!' etc. Perhaps the offender would be reprieved, owing to the (exaggerated) terror on his face, and sentence be commuted to the Head's favourite charity. 'Do you agree to pay tuppence to the Fresh Air Fund, sir? You do. Put Williamson's name down for tuppence, Latymer. Next time, sir, you will not get off so lightly. You are the worst boy in the school, sir!'

INDIAN SUMMER NOTEBOOK

But he was not always the falcon stooping upon lesser birds who could not emulate his flight and vision. He was courtesy itself to those pleading headaches, toothaches, earaches, etc. Many did, to excuse lack of preparation. I discovered a rare bird, then almost unknown, during a 'visit to the dentist' in the Fox Grove Woods at Beckenham – a willow titmouse.

In my own eyes, without undue concern, I knew myself to be a coward, poor at games, an idiot at Euclid, etc. etc. I left just before the Great War arose in my mind with excitement and fear and secret hope that it would not subside into peace, on that blue and sunlit August Bank Holiday of 1914. If I was the worst boy, the most brilliant scholar, who in my second year at the Heath School (to give it its original name) went on to Rugby, was the Head Master's son, F.L. Lucas, now a don at Cambridge. He was older than I, but I remember my admiration for his achievement, which was to head the Senior Cambridge Local list throughout Great Britain for the year, with First Class Honours and distinctions in many subjects, including Greek. I can still see him standing by the parallel bars in Big Hall, after the Lists had come and the Head had said: 'Now you shall know your fates!' as he stood modestly outside the Sixth Form room, his blue eyes lowered in the sensitive face of a poet.

My tears have been clouds these many decades; my hate, or strangled love, was never strong. 'The Old Bird', I have often thought, took on a heroic task; he should not have worn himself out in a London suburban school of 300 boys, but have been a tutor at, soon surely to have become Master of, one of the colleges at the ancient Universities; for his mental range was wide and he lived to instil and to pass on his abiding love of the flowers of our western civilisation, based on 'the radiance of Hellas'. I remember him with affection, as I remember most of the faces of my time at the school, including the hundred or so of my generation who were killed in the 1914-18 War.

Contribution to *John Bull's Schooldays*, edited by Brian Inglis
Hutchinson, 1961

The Christmas Truce

THE First Battle of Ypres was over. The deluge in the second week of November 1914 decided that. Our battalion of the London Regiment (Territorials) was out at rest, leaving a memory of dead soldiers in *feld grau* (field grey) and khaki lying in still attitudes between the German and British lines. 'Rest' meant no more fatigues or carrying parties; it meant letters from home, parcels, hazy nights in the *estaminets* of Hazebrouck with *café-rhum* and weak beer, clouds of smoke and noisy laughter.

After 48 hours clear, a daily route march, leading to nowhere and back again, with new faces of the drafts which had come up from the base. The war was now a mere rumour from afar: a low-flashing, dull booming beyond an eastern horizon of flat, tree-lined and arable fields gleaming with water in cart-rut and along each furrow.

In the first week of December 1914 the King Emperor George V arrived at St Omer in northern France, headquarters of the British Expeditionary Force. Orders were given immediately at all units to prepare for a royal inspection.

The King, in the service uniform of a field-marshal, brown-booted with gold spurs, brown-bearded, prominent pouches under his blue eyes, passed with Field-Marshal Sir John French and various general staff officers down the ranks of silent, staring-ahead, depersonalised faces thinking that the gruff tones in which the King spoke to the commander-in-chief were of that other world infinitely remote from what really happened.

Behind the King walked the Prince of Wales, seeming somehow detached from the massive power of red and gold, the big moustaches and faces and belts and boots and spurs all so shining and immaculate between the open ranks of the troops standing rigidly at attention. The slim figure of the Prince, in the uniform of a Grenadier, appeared to be looking for something far beyond the immediate scene – a slight, white-faced boy in the shadow of Father.

The next afternoon the platoon sergeant walked from billet to billet, with orders that we were going into the line that evening. A waning moon rode the sky, memento of *estaminet* nights, moon-silvered cobble stones, colour-washed house-fronts of the *Grande Place*. The decaying orb was ringed by scudding vapour; a wet wind flapped the edges of rubber groundsheets fastened over packs and shoulders of the marching men. A wind from the south-west brought rain to the brown, the flat, the tree-lined plain of Flanders.

Going back was by now a prospect of stoical acceptance, since marching in the rain absorbed all personal memory, leaving little for coherent thought beyond the moment. We marched along a road lined with poplars towards the familiar hazy pallor thrown on low clouds by the ringed lights around Ypres – called 'Ypriss' by the old sweats who had been out since Mons. As we came nearer, the sky was tremulous with flashes: the night burdened by reverberation of cannon heard with the lisp of rainy wind in the bare branches of trees above our heads.

At last we halted, and welcome news arrived. The company was in reserve. We were to be billeted for the night in some sheds, and thatched lofts around a farm. Speculation ceased when the platoon commander said that we were taking over part of the line the following evening. The Germans, he said, had attacked down south; the battalion was to remain in the brigade reserve. It was a quiet part of the line. There was to be diversionary fire from the trenches, to relieve the pressure.

'Cushy,' we said among ourselves as we entered our cottage, to sleep upon the floor. There was a large stove, radiating heat. *Bon* for the troops!

The damp December dusk of next evening was closing down as No. 1 Company approached the dark mass of leafless trees at the edge of a wood. Through the trees lay a novel kind of track, firm but knobbly to the feet, but so welcome after the mud of the preceding field. It was like walking on an uneven and wide ladder. Rough rungs, laid close together, were made of little, sawn-off branches, nailed to laid trunks of oak trees. As we came near to the greenish-white German flares, bullets began to crack. The men of the new draft ducked at each overhead crack; but the survivors of the original battalion walked on upright, sometimes muttering, 'Don't get the wind-up, chum,' as the old sweats had said to them when first they had gone into the line, many weeks before.

THE CHRISTMAS TRUCE

We came to a cross-ride in the wood, and waited there, while a cock-pheasant crowed as it flew past us. Dimly seen were some bunkers, in which braziers glowed brightly. The sight was homely, and cheering. Figures in balaclava woollen helmets stood about.

'What's it like, mate?' came the inevitable question. 'Cushy,' came the reply, as a cigarette brightened. These were regulars, the newcomers felt happy again. Braziers, lovely crackling coke flames!

The relief company filed on down the path, and came to the luminous edge of the wood, beyond which the German parachute flares were clear and bright, like lilies. The trench was just inside the wood. There was no water in it, thank God! One saw sandbag-dugouts behind the occupants standing by for the relief. It was indeed cushy!

Thus began a period or cycle of eight days for No. 1 Company: two in the front line followed by two days back in battalion reserve in billets, two in support within the wood and two more again in the front line. It was not unenjoyable: danger was negligible – a whizz-bang arriving now and again – object more of curiosity than of fear – news of someone getting sniped; work in the trench, digging by day, revetting the parapet, and fatigues in the wood by night; for the weather remained fine. One trench had a well-made parapet with steel loopholes built in the sandbags, and paved along a length of 50 yards entirely by unopened tins of bully-beef taken from some of the hundreds of boxes lying about in the wood. These boxes had been chucked away by former carrying parties, in the days before 'corduroy' paths. The trench had been built by the regulars, now no longer bearded, though some of their toes showed through their boots. It was said that a cigarette end, dropped somewhere along it, was a 'crime' heavily punished.

All form, and shape even, of the carefully-made trenches disappeared under rains falling upon the yellow clay which retained them. One was soaked all day and all night. The weight of a greatcoat was doubled by clay and water. 'We volunteered for this!' was an ironic comment among those in water sometimes to the waist.

After the rains, mist lay over a countryside which had no soul, with its broken farmhouse roofs, dead cattle in no man's land, its daylight nihilism beyond the parapet with never a movement of life, never a glimpse of the Alleyman (*Allemand* – German) – except those who were dead, and lying motionless in varying attitudes of stillness day after day upon the level brown field extending to the yellow subsoil thrown up from the enemy trench, beyond its barbed wire obstacles. At night mist blurred the brightness of the light-balls, the Véry lights or flares as they were now generally called. The mists, hanging heavier in the wood, settled to hoar, which rimed trees, corduroy paths, shed and barn; and clarified into keener air in sunlight. Frost formed floating films of ice upon the clay-blue water in shell-holes, which tipped when mess-tins were dipped for brewing tea; the daily ration of tea being mixed in sandbags with sugar. It was pleasant in the wood, squatting by a little stick fire. Movement was, however, laborious now upon the paths not yet laid with corduroy by the sappers. Boots became pattened with yellow clay. Still, we said, it might be worse – for memory of the tempest that had fallen on the last day of the battle for Ypres, of the misery of cold and wet, the dereliction of that time, was still in the forefront of our minds.

One afternoon, towards Christmas, a harder frost settled upon the vacant battlefield. By midnight trees, bunkers, paths, sentries' balaclavas and greatcoat shoulders became stiff, thickly rimed. From some of the new draft came suppressed whimpering sounds. Only those old soldiers who had scrounged sandbags and straw from Iniskilling Farm at one edge of the wood, and put their boots inside, lay still and sleeping. Lying with unprotected boots outside the open end of a bunker, one endured pain in one's feet until the final agony, when one got up and hobbled outside, seeing bright stars above the treetops. The thing to do was to make a fire, and boil some water in a mess-tin for some Nestlé's *café-au-lait*. There were many shell-fractured oak-branches lying about. They were heavy with sap, but no matter. One passed painful hours of sleeplessness in blowing and fanning weak embers amid a hiss of bubbling branch-ends.

As soon as I sat still, or stood up to beat my arms like a cabby on a hansom cab, the weak glow of the fire went dull. My eyes smarted with smoke, there was no flame unless I fanned all the time. My arms were heavy in the frozen greatcoat sleeves, mud-slabbed and hard as drainpipes; while the skirts of the coat were like boards. I went back to sleep, but pain kept me awake; so I crawled out again and was once more in frozen air, bullets smacking through trees glistening with frost. I was thirsty, but the water-bottle was solid. Later, when it was thawed out over a brazier, it leaked, being split, but there were many lying about in the wood, with rifles and other equipment.

THE CHRISTMAS TRUCE

We were issued with shaggy goatskin jerkins. Did it mean that the battalion was intended to be an Officers' Training Corps? That there would be no more attacks until the spring? The jerkins had broad tapes which cross-bound the white and yellow hairy skins against the chest. Officers and men now looked alike, except for the expression of an officer's face, and the fact that one appeared to stand more upright; an effect given, perhaps, by the shoulder-high thumbsticks of ash many of them walked about with.

Senior officers also wore Norwegian type knee-boots, laced to the knee and then treble-strapped. I thought of asking my father to send me a pair, but a thaw came at the beginning of the third week of December, and the misery of mud returned. And then, with a jump of concealed fear, orders were read out for an attack across no man's land to the German lines. It was two days after the new moon. We were in support. The company lay out on the edge of the wood, shivering and beating hands and feet, in support of a regular battalion of the Rifle Brigade. The objectives were a cottage in no man's land called Sniper's House, and thence forward to a section of the enemy front line that enfiladed our dangerous T-trench.

The assault of muttering and tense-faced bearded men took place under a serried rank of bursting red stars of 18-pounder shrapnel shells, and supporting machine gun fire. Figures floundering across a root-field in no man's land, with its sad decaying lumps of cows and men. Hoarse yells of fear became simulated rage; while short of, into and beyond the British front line dropped shell upon shell to burst with acrid yellow fumes of lyddite from the British Long-toms of the South African war of 1902, with their worn rifling.

The order came for the company to carry on the attack. Survivors, coming back through the wood, wet through and covered with mud, uniforms ripped by barbed wire, were stumbling as they passed through us. When they had gone away – away from the line, death behind them – a clear baritone voice floated back through the trees, singing *Oh, for the wings, for the wings of a dove – far away, far away would I roam.* They were wonderful, remarked a sergeant, a rugger-playing Old Blue in peacetime. Yes, because they were going out, I thought; they were euphoric, hurrying to warmth and sleep, sleep, sleep.

This local attack failed on the uncut German wire; but Sniper's House was taken. Our colonel, one heard later, had protested against the carrying on of the attack by our company. Later, it was reported in 'Comic Cuts', or Corps Intelligence sheets, that the attack had been ordered to aid the Russians, hard pressed on the Eastern front. We laughed sceptically at that; a beginning of disillusionment with 'the well-fed Staff'.

I had no fear at night, and used to wander about in no man's land by myself, to feel some sort of freedom. One night I was sitting down by the German wire when a flare hissed out just by my face, it seemed, followed by another, and another, while machine guns opened up with loud directness, accompanied by the cracking air-shear of bullets passing only a few inches, it seemed, above my neck. Then up and down the line arose the swishing stalks of white lights, all from the German lines, by which one knew that they were not going to attack, but feared an assault from our lines. This was remote comfort, as I felt myself to be large and visible, sweating with fear of sorts, while bullets from our lines thudded and whanged away upwards in ricochet. The sky above me appeared to be lit by the beautiful white lilies of the dead, as I thought of them.

This was an occasion of that phenomenon known as wind-up. As before a wind, fire swept with bright yellow-red stabs of thorn-flame up the line towards the light-ringed salient around Ypres: bullets in flight, hissing, clacking or whining, crossed the lines of the hosts of the unburied dead slowly being absorbed into Flanders field. The wind of fear, the nightly wind of the battlefield of Western Europe, from the cold North Sea to the great barrier of the Alps – a fire travelling faster than any wind, was speckling the ridges above the drained marsh that surrounded Ypres, stabbing in wandering aimless design the darkness on the slopes of the Commines canal, running in thin crenellations upon the plateau of Wytschaete and Messines, sweeping thence down to the plain of Armentières, among the coal-mines and slags of Artois, across the chalk uplands of Picardy, and the plains of the rivers. The wind of fear rushed on, to die out, expended, beyond the dark forest of the Argonne, beyond the fears of massed men, where snow-field, ravine, torrent and crag ended before the peaks in silence under the constellation of Orion, shaking gem-like above all human hope.

It was still freezing hard on Christmas Eve. We had been detailed for what seemed to be a perilous fatigue in no man's land – going out between the lines to knock in posts in a zigzag line towards the

German front line. Around the posts wire was to be wound. On this wire, hurdles taken from a shed were to be laid. Then drying tobacco leaves, hung on the hurdles (as the leaves had been in the shed), would give cover from view should it be necessary, in an attack, to reinforce the front line.

What an idea, I thought. It would draw machine gun fire. It was about as sensible as the brigade commander's idea for the December 19 attack across no man's land, for some men to carry straw palliasses, to lean against the German wire and enable men to cross over the entanglements. As for the knocking-in of posts into frozen ground, that was utterly wrong! And in bright moonlight, 40 yards away from the Alleyman!

After our platoon commander, a courteous man in his early 20s and fresh from Cambridge, had outlined the plan quietly, he asked for questions. I dared to say that the noise of knocking in posts would be heard. There was silence; then we were told that implicit directions had come from brigade, and must be carried out. We debouched from the wood, and were exposed. After an initial stab of fear, I was not afraid. Everything was so still, so quiet in the line. No flares, no crack of the sniper's rifle. No gun firing.

Soon we were used to the open moonlight in which all life and movement seemed unreal. Men were fetching and laying down posts, arranging themselves in couples, one to hold, the other to knock. Others prepared to unwind barbed wire previously rolled on staves. I was one who followed the platoon commander and three men to a tarred wooden shed, to fetch hurdles hung with long dry tobacco leaves, which we brought out and laid on the site of the reinforcement fence.

And not a shot was fired from the German trench. The unbelievable had soon become the ordinary, so that we talked as we worked, without caution, while the night passed as in a dream. The moon moved down to the treetops behind us. Always, it seemed, had we been moving bodilessly, each with his shadow.

After a timeless dream I saw what looked like a large white light on top of a pole put up in the German lines. It was a strange sort of light. It burned almost white, and was absolutely steady. What sort of lantern was it? I did not think much about it; it was part of the strange unreality of the silent night, of the silence of the moon, now turning a brownish yellow, of the silence of the frost mist. I was warm with the work, all my body was in glow, not with warmth but with happiness.

Suddenly there was a short quick cheer from the German lines – *Hoch! Hoch! Hoch!* With others I flinched and crouched, ready to fling myself flat, pass the leather thong of my rifle over my head and aim to fire; but no other sound came from the German lines.

We stood up, talking about it, in little groups. For other cheers were coming across the black spaces of no man's land. We saw dim figures on the enemy parapet, about more lights; and with amazement saw that a Christmas tree was being set there, and around it Germans were talking and laughing together. *Hoch! Hoch! Hoch!*, followed by cheering.

Our platoon commander, who had gone from group to group during the making of the fence, looked at his watch and told us that it was eleven o'clock. One more hour, he said, and then we would go back.

'By Berlin time it is midnight. A Merry Christmas to you all! I say, that's rather fine, isn't it?', for from the German parapet a rich baritone voice had begun to sing a song I remembered from my nurse Minne singing it to me after my evening tub before bed. She had been maid to my German grandmother, one of the Lune family of Hildesheim. *Stille Nacht! Heilige Nacht!*

Tranquil Night! Holy Night! The grave and tender voice rose out of the frozen mist; it was all so strange; it was like being in another world, to which one had come through a nightmare: a world finer than the one I had left behind me in England, except for beautiful things like music, and springtime on my bicycle in the countryside of Kent and Bedfordshire.

And back again in the wood it seemed so strange that we had not been fired upon; wonderful that the mud had gone; wonderful to walk easily on the paths; to be dry; to be able to sleep again.

The wonder remained in the low golden light of a white-rimed Christmas morning. I could hardly realise it; but my chronic, hopeless longing to be home was gone.

The post arrived while I was frying my breakfast bacon, beside a twig fire where stood my canteen full of hot sugary tea. I sat on an unopened 28-lb box of 2-ounce Capstan tobacco: one of scores thrown down in the wood, with large bright metal containers of army biscuits, of the shape and size and taste of dog biscuits. The tobacco issue per day was reckoned to be 5,000 cigarettes at this time, or 24 lbs of tobacco. This was not the 'issue' ration, but from the many 'Comforts for the Troops' appeals in newspapers, all tobacco being duty free to our benefactors at home.

There was a Gift Package to every soldier from the Princess Royal. A brass box embossed with Princess Mary's profile, containing tobacco and cigarettes. This I decided to send home to my mother, as a souvenir.

'There's bloody hundreds of them out there!' said a kilted soldier to me as I sat there.

I walked through the trees, some splintered and gashed by fragments of Jack Johnsons, as we called the German 5.9-inch gun, and into no man's land and found myself face to face with living German soldiers, men in grey uniforms and leather knee-boots – a fact which was at the time for me beyond belief. Moreover the Germans were, some of them, actually smiling as they talked in English.

Most of them were small men, rather pale of face. Many wore spectacles, and had thin little goatee beards. I did not see one *pickelhaube*. They were either bare-headed, or had on small grey pork-pie hats, with red bands. Each bore two metal buttons, ringed with white, black and red rather like tiny archery targets: the Imperial German colours.

Among these smaller Saxons were tall, sturdy men taking no part in the talking, but regarding the general scene with detachment. They were red-faced men and their tunics and trousers above the leather knee-boots showed dried mud marks. Some had green cords round a shoulder, and under the shoulder tabs.

Looking in the direction of the mass of Germans, I saw, judging by the serried rows of figures standing there, at least three positions or trench lines behind the front trench. They were dug at intervals of about 200 yards.

'It only shows,' said one of our chaps, 'what a lot of men they have, compared to our chaps. We've only got one line, really, the rest are mere scratches.' He said quietly, 'See those green lanyards and tassels on that big fellow's shoulders? They're sniper's cords. They're Prussians. That's what some Saxons told me. They dislike the Prussians. "Kill them all," said one, "and we'll have peace".'

'Yes, my father was always against the Prussians,' I told him. One of the small Saxons was contentedly standing alone and smoking a new and large meerschaum pipe. He wore spectacles and looked like a comic-paper 'Hun'. The white bowl of the pipe bore the face and high-peaked cap of 'Little Willie' painted on it. The Saxon saw me looking at it and taking pipe from mouth said with quiet satisfaction: '*Kronprinz! Prächtiger Kerl!*' before putting back the mouthpiece carefully between his teeth.

Someone told me that *Prächtiger Kerl* meant 'Good Chap' or 'Decent Fellow'. Of course, I thought, he is to them as the Prince of Wales is to us.

A mark of German efficiency I noted: two aluminium buttons where we had one brass button on our trousers. Men were digging, to bury stiff corpses. Each *feld grau* 'stiffy' was covered by a red-black-white German flag. When the grave had been filled in an officer read from a prayer-book, while the men in *feld grau* stood to attention with round grey hats clutched in left hands. I found myself standing to attention, my balaclava in my hand. When the grave was filled, someone wrote, in indelible pencil, these words on the rough cross of ration-box wood: *Hier Ruht In Gott Ein Unbekannter Deutscher Held.* 'Here rests in God an unknown German hero', I found myself translating: and thinking that it was like the English crosses in the little cemetery in the clearing within the wood.

I learned, with surprise, that the German assaults in mass attack through the woods and across the arable fields of the salient, during the last phase of the Battle for Ypres, had been made by young volunteers, some arm in arm, singing, with but one rifle to every three. They had been 'flung in' (as the British military term went) after the failure of the Prussian Guard, the élite *Corps du Garde*, modelled on Napoleon's famous soldiers, to break our line. And here was the surprise: 'You had too many *automatische pistolen* in your line, *Englische* friend!'

As a fact, we had few if any machine guns left after the battle; the Germans had mistaken their presence for our 'fifteen rounds rapid' fire! Every infantry battalion had been equipped with two machine guns, of the type used in the South African War of 1902; with one exception. That was the London Scottish, the 14th Battalion of the London Regiment, which had bought, privately before the war, two Vickers guns. These also were lost during the battle.

Another illusion of the Germans appeared to be that we had masses of reserve troops behind our front line, most of them in the woods. If only they had known that we had very few reserves, including some of the battalions of an Indian Division, the turbanned soldiers of which suffered greatly from the cold.

The truce lasted, in our part of the line (under the Messines Ridge), for several days. On the last day of 1914, one evening, a message came over no man's land, carried by a very polite Saxon corporal. It was that their regimental (equivalent to our brigade, but they had three battalions where we had four) staff officers were going round their line at midnight; and they would have to fire their *automatische pistolen*, but would aim high, well above our heads. Would we, even so, please keep under cover, 'lest regrettable accidents occur'.

And at 11 o'clock – for they were using Berlin time – we saw the flash of several Spandau machine guns passing well above no man's land.

I had taken the addresses of two German soldiers, promising to write to them after the war. And I had, vaguely, a childlike idea that if all those in Germany could know what the soldiers had to suffer, and that both sides believed the same things about the righteousness of the two national causes, it might spread, this truce of Christ on the battlefield, to the minds of all, and give understanding where now there was scorn and hatred.

I was still very young. I was under age, having volunteered after the news of the Retreat from Mons had come to us one Sunday in the third week of August 1914. Our colonel had made a speech to the battalion, then in London, declaring that the British Expeditionary Force of the Regular army was very reduced in numbers after the 90-mile retreat which had worn out boots and exhausted so many, and was in dire need of help.

And now the New Year had come, the frost was settling again in little crystals upon posts and on the graves and icy shell holes in no man's land. Once more the light-balls were rising up to hover under little parachutes over no man's land with the blast of machine guns, and the brutal downward droning of heavy shells. And the rains came, to fall upon Flanders field, while preparations were in hand for the spring offensive.

Contribution to *History of the First World War*, Vol. 2, no.4
Purnell & Sons, 1970

When I Was Demobilised

I AND my friends and others of our generation went into the war in a state of excitement and left it in a state of vacancy bordering on disillusion.

Perhaps I was more eccentric than most; for I had gone to the front in 1914, very young, to see action before my eighteenth birthday; and while trench-life at first had been exciting, and even enjoyable, nothing I had heard or read or been told had prepared me for the reality of men in battle.

When I came home a few months later, after some time in hospital, I was treated as a hero, on the basis that the enemy was stupid, cowardly, and always ran away from our heroic selves. Any attempt to stammer the truth was at once regarded as modesty; later, as unpatriotic. Civilians saw the war from newspapers; and what the man from the actual fighting tried to say was not acceptable.

So the two worlds drew apart; the world of the soldier was different from the mental sphere of the civilian. A schism arose, which was not closed again (and then only superficially) until Remarque's *All Quiet on the Western Front* swept the reading public of all nations in 1928.

The book was an exaggeration, the work of a war-haunted German youth who had not experienced all that he wrote about; it sold five million copies.

I left the Army in the summer following the armistice. I was then with the reserve battalion at Cannock Chase, and I had done with the war. I had discovered myself as a writer, and spent my days in my asbestos cubicle writing, and reading Galsworthy, Shakespeare, Shelley, and Richard Jefferies.

I was immensely exhilarated by the world I had discovered my true self to be part of. I wanted to write the truth as I had seen it, and to do this it was necessary to keep myself entirely apart from my fellows. Parades, what were parades? I had done with parades!

So I stayed in my cubicle, eating biscuits and making tea, and occasionally going into mess dinner at night. I knew nobody there, and avoided speaking to them, as to strangers. I had a racing motor-cycle, the first post-war model turned out by a famous Birmingham firm, and sometimes went to Stratford to buy food, and meet acquaintances in the bars of hotels.

After two or three weeks of such irregular conduct, during which time I had ignored all chits summoning me to the orderly room, from both assistant adjutant and adjutant – both junior in service to myself – I was sent for by the colonel. He said curtly that I must hand in my papers.

He had been through the war from the beginning, and so I apologised to him for my conduct. He said he was glad I had apologised; and then I told him, in halting words, that I was possessed by an overwhelming feeling to devote myself to writing. We shook hands, while my eyes could not see properly; and the next day I left on my motor-cycle for London and demobilisation. A few formalities at the Crystal Palace, and I was out again, a free man.

It was then that I felt lost; all my years since boyhood – a very long time to me – the Army had been my home, indeed it had been my entire grown-up world. Now I had no world, except the shadowy and diminished sphere of civvy life which had been steadily dissolving since 1914. I could hardly speak to my parents; there were hardly any light-rays between our worlds.

I remember going slowly round the streets of Sydenham, wondering what I could do. At last I went to London, to stay in an hotel and visit some of my war-time leave-haunts. But I might have been a ghost. I drank beer alone, yet with imaginary comrades.

The next day I went to the Army bankers to see about my 'blood-money', or gratuity. This was payable at the rate of 180 days' pay for the first year of commissioned service, with 90 days' pay for every subsequent year or part of a year. I found I had nearly £300 to come. Of this, £100 had already been spent on the racing motor-cycle.

I wrote at night, and loafed about during the day. I ran into some of my friends and we hailed one another with cries of happiness. One was thinking of starting a poultry farm in Suffolk; another wanted to raise a loan to supplement his gratuity and buy a tractor to do contract ploughing in Essex.

A third wanted to be an actor; he had been a great success on guest nights in the past, with monologues accompanied with music from a home-made cigar-box violoncello. He told us of Major X, a ranker who had won both DSO and DCM, being seen outside a picture palace in the uniform of a commissionaire.

Another, a rather wild fellow who was an artist of sorts before the war, was going round the West End wearing a mask and uniform without rank-badges or buttons, and playing a barrel-organ.

It was a strange world; but the lighted bars at night, which we haunted, gave us a feeling of war-time comradeship. What did the future matter? It had never mattered in the only world we knew, that of the war.

There was an ex-Officers' Association, to which I and a friend went, putting down our names for jobs. Any jobs; at home or abroad. We learned that what we were in the Army was of little use in the new world we were now becoming accustomed to.

One of my friends was offered a job as clerk in a shirt-factory in the East End. Later he went to South Africa, on a Government scheme, farming. I heard from him once only; he must have lost out when the slump came, later on.

Gradually we drifted apart. The new world took us our different ways. I don't say that all were like ourselves; I can speak only of my little clique, made up of chaps a little less steady than the majority. One of them, a polished youth with charming manners and considerable skill at bridge, who had somehow wangled himself a job as ADC to a divisional commander, had managed to stay out of the fighting all through.

He was a young man of great charm, who had built for himself a bogus background during the war. Some of his letters in the mess had been addressed to Capt. the Honble. Charles Y——; we thought at the time he had written them to himself.

I remember him returning from draft leave once with a gift of pheasants for the MO (he had been returned to duty from his red-tab job in 1918, after a severe comb-out following the vast losses of Third Ypres). He went sick, after giving the birds to the reserve battalion doctor, saying they were from his 'place in the country'. He got off the draft.

A year or two later, I read in a newspaper that the charming Captain Y—— was one of a gang of cardsharpers and gamblers taken in a West End 'haunt'. There were several other charges, all from living on his wits. With a little more sincerity this pre-war bank clerk might have made a name for himself as an actor. He went to prison for two years.

WHEN I WAS DEMOBILISED

Gradually we were absorbed into the post-war. The battlefields were cleared up. Tens of thousands of Poles and Italians filled in the craters with long-handled shovels; tens of thousands of tons of rusty dud shells and fragments of steel were collected into dumps.

We used to say during the war that it would take a hundred years to clear up the Somme battlefields; actually it was done in little more than half a hundred months. As for the human souls that once trudged there, in sweat and terror, in cold and mud and in heat and choking dust, they, too, became in time indistinguishable from the civilian world of which they had once been so derisive.

Once a year we met at a regimental dinner, and spoke, in odd sentences, almost in shyness, of our vanished world of comradeship. Every year the dinner was more sparsely attended; until one day a circular came from the honorary secretary of the Old Comrades Association, saying that it was decided to discontinue the yearly meeting.

So it came about that I left London and went to live in a cottage in Devon by myself, to meditate and to write the truth as I saw it, to clarify what we fought and died for – a new vision of the world. As the years went on I saw that vision receding, and the shadows stealing forth again towards those who had not been born when I was a soldier of 1914-18.

Is the vision lost? Somehow I think that the new post-war generation, when its authentic voice is heard, will join in comradeship with those who went before.

Contribution to *Strand Magazine*
September, 1945

Richard Jefferies

Richard Jefferies was a poor man who in moments of inspiration believed himself to be a prophetic thinker and writer of the world. The world did not think so. He was born in 1848, and he died in 1887, aged thirty-eight years. During the later part of his life he was ill as well as poor; and two years before his death, he lived in perpetual agony. Some doctors thought his illness was imaginary, that he was a hypochondriac, that the wasting away of his body and the perpetual pains he suffered were due to hysteria. Actually he suffered from tuberculosis of the lungs and intestines, and the intestines were ulcerated as well. Also he had fistula, which is a most torturing thing. All during his life he was working: and the theme of his work was the creation of, the burning hope for, a better, truer, more sunlit world of men.

Richard Jefferies was the son of a Wiltshire farmer. He was a genius, a visionary whose thought and feeling were wide as the human world, prophet of an age not yet come into being – the age of sun, of harmony. He was derided in his father's house, upbraided for idleness and stupidity; considered 'looney' by the neighbours. Since a man can truly be friends with his peers only, Jefferies was friendless to his life's end.

During his boyhood and youth he lived at Coate Farm, in the parish of Chisledon, near Swindon. The farm lay under the chalk downs. Behind the farmhouse were trees, and then a broad sheet of water, with reeds and rushes and wildfowl, and two islets near the shore. Pike lived in there, with roach and rudd and perch, and other fish. From his boyhood memories of this place the best boys' book in England was written; *Bevis: the Story of a Boy*.

After his death, there was some controversy about whether or no he died a Christian. His life's work was indignantly attacked in the *Girls' Own Paper*. This was stupid; and it was wicked. Stupidity is the same thing as wickedness, or the devil, to this modern age of half-sun. It was wicked because it denied and persecuted the truth of heaven.

RICHARD JEFFERIES

During his lifetime Jefferies had to fight against much ununderstanding; and it wore him to an early death.

The affinity of Jefferies with Jesus of Nazareth is patent in nearly all his work. If Francis of Assisi is a little brother of the birds, Jefferies of Wiltshire is a little brother of Jesus, of the sun, of clarity, of all things fine and natural and designed and efficient. Jefferies saw with paradise-clearness.

The century that slew him passed away, and still he remained insufficiently esteemed. The following is typical. Thirty-three years after his death, when I was a reporter in Fleet Street, I was talking to an old literary gentleman about Jefferies. It was in Carmelite House, then the home of Lord Northcliffe's newspapers. It was a wearing life, for men of sensibility. The old chap was a special writer for an evening paper; he was a scholar whose writings were famous to a small circle only, and to first-edition collectors. He was always violently bitter about the British public. 'Don't try and write for a living; keep pigs,' was his immediate reply to the young aspirant who approached him timidly in the little room, always lit by artificial light, where he worked. He waved hand and arm in a sweep of derision of the whole building. Then he began rolling Latin verse off his tongue. His tie was always askew around his tall 1890 collar. Red-faced, big-headed, he looked like a monk with his long white bobbed hair almost touching the shoulders of his cloak. I felt it a privilege to hear this famous writer talk like that. I had bought some of his books, but had dipped into them only, and never finished them. The famous prose seldom stood out of the pages. One day, meeting him again in the corridor, I dared to ask if he liked the works of Richard Jefferies. 'Jefferies? A mere cataloguer of sights and sounds,' he replied, and had nothing more to say, and I knew then what I had suspected, that he had not that *something* that marks out a writer of genius from the writer who is scholarly, pretentious, literary, whose work is a gilt of borrowed gold, imitation of poetic vision. (This was probably youthful intolerance: for he was a passionate writer.) When I saw him coming along a passage, I used to turn away and hide. He had called my Jefferies a 'mere cataloguer'.

During the sixteen years that passed since the advice to keep pigs (advice which I am ready to take now) I collected various opinions of Jefferies by other writers, with the intention of quoting them in a book on his work, to show why those derogatory or disprizing remarks were merely an indication of a lack in the writers themselves: such lack going hand-in-hand with their non-success as writers with the general public. But it is not worth doing. The works of D.H. Lawrence, another writer who has much in common with Jefferies, contain many portraits of his detractors or non-appreciators, all of them arising from Lawrence's own tortured sensibility. Such writing is a mistake. It is not truly creative. The writer should shine on his characters with the serenity of the sun.

Jefferies was born two, perhaps three, generations before his time. In May 1925, nearly forty years after his death, I made a journey to his birthplace, and stared at the farmhouse where he had been born, at the gable window from which he had looked when writing his first pages. I walked round the broad or lake, and thought how much smaller it was than in *Bevis*. It had been made into a public bathing-place, with huts and rails and diving boards; but the fish were still there. There was talk of turning the farmhouse into a Jefferies museum, for a memorial. Soon nothing, I thought, would be left of the place as he knew it, except in those pages of his which glowed and shone with ancient sunlight. While I was musing thus, standing in the roadway before the farm, an old woman came out of a small cot of tarred wood, obviously the work of a labouring man, and scrutinised me. The little black house stood under a hawthorn, then in pink blossom. 'Come to see the house where Loony Dick was born, have ye?' she enquired. We talked for some time. She was remarkable for her vivacity and straight way of looking at things. Years before the War she had adopted a foundling or waif from the Union or workhouse; raised him as her own child, found him a job when grown up; and then the war came, and killed him. What she could not make up her mind about at the moment, she told me, was whether or no to adopt another 'chiel'. There were plenty of 'm about, she declared, since the soldiers had gone. Was she too old, did I think? I said surely not, that she had many years to live. Don't ye be too sure, she said, and defied me to guess her age. Sixty? I said. 'Git out,' she replied, 'I knew Loony Dick as a boy, didn't I tell 'ee just now? Moony Dick, some called him. A lazy loppet, he was, too. A proper atheist. Lots of folks asks me if I have read those books. Why should I read them? I know it all as well as he. He can't tell me anything new. I've had to work all my life. Why should I read in books what most folks knows already?'

RICHARD JEFFERIES

(After his death, a relative wrote of Jefferies as a boy, 'Dick was of a masterful temperament, and though less strong than several of us in a bodily sense, his force of will was such that we had to succumb to whatever plans he chose to dictate, never choosing to be second even in the most trivial thing . . .')

All the strain and desperation in much of Jefferies' writings, and his sickness and premature death, can be traced to the human surroundings of his childhood, youth, and early manhood. Those who called him, to his face, Loony Dick, or Lazy Loppet, who laughed at his aspirations and derided his early efforts to be a writer, were to him so narrow and warped and ruined that he could say nothing to them. The poor boy with the instincts of an aristocrat shut himself away from them; he lived in books and wandered on the downs, spreading himself in the air and grass and sky until he was recharged with vitality and hope, and made eager once again for a fuller, a happier life for all the warped and ruined human minds he saw about him in both the slums of Swindon and his own hamlet.

After he had left school, the young Jefferies, a mixture of indolence and sharp imperiousness, got a job on a local paper, the *North Wilts Herald*. At night he wrote novels and romances in the seclusion of the gable room, which had a pear tree trained against the outer wall. *Caesar Borgia, or the King of Crime*; *Verses on the Exile of the Prince Imperial*; *Fortune, or the Art of Success* (he sent this to Disraeli, who returned it with a tactfully insincere letter); *Only a Girl* – how he worked, burning candle after candle beyond midnight and into dawn.

Work on a country newspaper is good training for a young writer. There is not the hurried pressure and thwarting of nervous energy as in supplying small and often silly news stories for Fleet Street newspapers; there is no perpetual callousing and humiliation of feelings, no distortion of truth in the manufacture of 'news'. A country newspaper is usually tactful, kindly, and its detail truthful. The meticulous gathering of names and facts of the little things of country life – the more names the better for the circulation of the newspaper – may be dull at times; but it is not degrading. And the young Jefferies was fortunate in having a sympathetic editor who believed that his young reporter had a distinct talent for writing.

His second editor's belief was justified when, at the age of twenty-four, Jefferies wrote a long letter to *The Times* in London; and *The Times* printed it in full, several thousand words, about the Wiltshire labourer. It was read and discussed in Swindon; the writer became a local figure. His chance! He found himself, suddenly, to be an authority in agriculture.

Imagine the tall, loose-limbed young man striding home from Swindon, paler than usual, the large blue eyes in the softly brown bearded face almost lifeless in the reaction of excitement, entering his father's house with an added lassitude of his drooping mouth and narrow shoulders, to stand about, silently, almost dully, and say casually, 'My letter's in.' 'What letter, Dick?' asks his mother, ironing on the kitchen table. 'In the paper.' 'The *Standard*? It's early this week, isn't it?' 'No, not that. I mean *The Times*.' His mother glances at it, and puts it down, while her son waits like a hawk for what she will not say. She says she is too busy just now, but will read it later; and he goes up into his room beside the cheese loft, and flops down in his chair, and feels more desperately than ever the awful deadness and dullness of house life and 'civilised' people. They will never understand. After supper he has violent indigestion, and cannot write a word of the new novel.

But he has begun. One day they will know what their son *is*.

In those days, before compulsory schooling taught nearly everyone to read, there were in England newspapers and periodicals which were written almost entirely by knowledgeable, or professional, writers. Among them were *Fraser's Magazine, The New Quarterly, The Standard, The Graphic, The Pall Mall Gazette, The Fortnightly, The Gentleman's Magazine, Longman's Magazine, The National Review, The English Illustrated Magazine,* and others. The editors of these papers and magazines, attracted by the letter in *The Times*, began to ask for and to print Jefferies' essays. A London evening newspaper, *The Pall Mall Gazette*, published a series of his articles, anonymously, under the title of *The Gamekeeper at Home, or, Sketches of Natural History and Rural Life*; and then another series, *Wild Life in a Southern County*. When these were reprinted in book form, the author was acclaimed as a writer in the class of White of Selbourne, and a public of discriminating sportsmen and country people began to look out for everything he wrote.

He was married now, to the daughter of a neighbouring farmer, and had a son. After the wedding the young couple had lived at Coate Farm, but soon found that life there was not possible; the ideas of the old people smothered the inspiration of the young author. So they took rooms in Swindon. Then, to be nearer editors, they moved to the suburbs of London, first to Sydenham and then to Surbiton. He worked every day; and the work of this period was always on a high level – informative and of the authentic countryside. Sometimes it was inclined to be static; for he had to write every day to support wife and family. It was then that other lesser writers began to use the label 'cataloguer'.

Most young writers who have had a sudden success ease up for a while, and thereby lose their form. Not so Jefferies. He wrote as before, novels and essays. In a recent critical appreciation of Jefferies, by a living writer who is also a Wiltshire man, I was shocked to read the opinion that all the Jefferies' novels could be 'thrown into the wastepaper basket'. But there are some beautiful things in the novels, even in the very early ones, when Jefferies was writing of scenes or incidents he had observed. Most of the early novels have scenes and characters based on what he had read in boyhood and youth; novels based on the fictional idiom of the day, and therefore blind or conventional writing. But among the novels are the exquisite *Greene Ferne Farm*, and *The Dewy Morn*, and *Amaryllis at the Fair*, one of the most lovely calm and balanced novels of country life and people in our literature. There is a naturalness, a bloom on *Amaryllis* which is not to be found in any of the novels of Hardy or the books of Hudson; and Hardy in the authenticity and detail of his country scenes is in the very rare first class with Shakespeare.

What is meant by the term 'very rare first class'? Let me try and explain this as a thing occurring in certain men and women; and why it occurs. This is only what one man thinks, remember; it may be true only in part, or it may be wholly wrong. Nevertheless, it may indicate why the lives of so many men of genius are tragic. This is my belief:—

The base or foundation of a first-class talent is eyesight. The man who sees more, who perceives quicker than his fellows, is of larger intelligence only by reason of that superior sight. Some people, educated unnaturally, seldom see for themselves; they don't know why things happen in the way they do: that every effect has a cause. An observant person is never stupid. Wisdom is the essence of observation.

The first-class writer always has first-class eyes. Often he is solitary from his companions in youth because they do not see so quickly or so widely as he does; and therefore do not think so quickly, or so plainly; and tend to ridicule what to them is not usual or ordinary.

It is as wretched for a slow-seeing person to be with a quick-seeing person, after the fact of difference has been established, as it is for the quick one to be with the slow one. Jefferies knew no one like himself, so he kept by himself. The derision and smallness of his fellows sealed him away from them; he was forced into solitude, where his enlarged and numerous faculties watched the actions of other life – clouds, grass, birds, fish, and natural men. He began to perceive why things happened; and reacted violently from conventional religion because it did not perceive how things happened. He judged religion by its ordinary exponents: the unintelligent mediocrity, men with minds spoiled in early life. In his lonely meditations on the downs he thought about the people in the houses and fields below and wondered how their lives could be made happier. In such solitude it was inevitable that he should strain to perceive or discover the meaning of life: to strain after that meaning, to try and force his thought through space to a definite meaning.

Later, the sight-records of what he had seen in those early days were used for reproduction on paper.

In the world of men speech came before writing: sound of words before sight of words. The first-rate writer always has a fine ear. He may be deaf in later life: but when young he must have *heard* acutely, as well as have *seen*, unconsciously to prepare the quality and substance of his writing. He writes by ear, balancing his sentences, sometimes automatically, but usually deliberately, for their *inner* music, which is the essence of life. It is an alchemic process, a spirit arising from a blend of transmuted sight-records and ear-records.

If you consider a moment, sight is responsible for almost all of the human world as it is today. So is sight the foundation of nearly all literature. (Mr. Robert Graves, himself a fine, austere poet, once declared that Keats had an unusually developed sense of taste – 'And lucent syrups tinct with cinnamon'.)

Some of the villagers in Ham, where I lived during the first decade after the World War, possessed copies of an old romantic novel with most of its scenes laid on the coast and country of North Devon. Someone lent me a copy, and I read first the descriptions of those places in the district I knew. They were accurate, and yet somehow they were insufficient, unsatisfying. It was not the style, which was no better and no worse than that of a hundred other novels of its period. The descriptions were somehow so bare, so colourless, although the fields were green, the sea was blue, the sands yellow, and so on. The book was pallid, un-sunned. In my youthful intolerance I scorned the book; until I learned that the author had been blind from birth.

All writing of the first class comes from exceptional sight and hearing: and insight arises from stored physical impressions of sight and sound. Those who observe quickly and vividly hold us with their detail, which is fresh and vivid; and they hold our attention because, being quick and vivid, their stories or pages have a flow which carries the reader. Now the rare first-class writer has, in addition to keen sight and hearing (it may be because of them), feelings or emotions which are equally keen. He has the keenness of a wild animal. He is natural. He is an authentic animation of the sun.

And because he is wild, natural, it is probable that he will be repressed and thwarted and made miserable in helpless childhood. This may cause him to be an ineffectual rebel, a liar, a bit of a thief, deceitful – if he has parents or mentors who, themselves victims of a repressive and unnatural upbringing, are without true or natural understanding and sympathy. Part of his natural integrity will thus be maimed; and that part will grow inwards, and perhaps mortify, and be the source of desperately sad resurrectional poetry and dream and vision later in life. This is what happened to Shelley, to Byron, to Francis Thompson, to Shakespeare (who outgrew his Hamlet), to Jefferies, to D.H. Lawrence, among many others in our literature.

It can be said of all of them, facilely, superficially, that they have a dual or multiple personality; but the truth, or cause, is as written above. Jefferies has two distinct styles. One of them is straightforward and concrete: the style of a natural man. The other is a candent, often incandescent, flow of words driven from him, as he wrote, by his dæmon (in Shelleyan language): the dæmon being his repressed or mortified self. It is this part of a man that strives to reach to God: the death, or mortification, in him striving to overcome his life.

Because of these two distinct styles, both of them authentic, Jefferies has two kinds of reading public. The one appreciates his straightforward descriptions of country scenes and characters, such as are to be found in *The Amateur Poacher*, *Wildlife in a Southern County*, and *Hodge and his Masters*; and this kind of reader does not like *The Story of my Heart* and the later essays wherein he wrote about himself and his own feelings. And there is the second kind of reader, who is pathologically akin to Jefferies, who prefers his introspective, sensuous writings to his matter-of-fact chapters.

It is always dangerous for a writer to write about himself and his own feelings; but when there is an intensity and power behind them, he produces a flow, a blend of sensuous records with emotion; and this is called poetry.

If circumstances or fate permit the metaphysical poet to outgrow the effects of his earlier mortifications, and through natural love accompanied by hard physical work (the natural life) to reassert himself to himself, he will become one of the rare first class, like Shakespeare, who, by virtue of his own experiences, real and imagined, understood all human actions and characters with clarity and the sweetness of truth. The rare first-class writer is then a universal representative of humanity, having attained wisdom by trial and error, by discarding parts of his earlier self through struggle and self-searching, and, above all, by self-criticism. So he achieves natural harmony: and thenceforward will have no regard for his writings – as a butterfly has no regard for the caterpillar – but wish only to live happily; and if he writes at all, will write only for money. Jefferies had just become a writer of the rare first class when the struggle broke him.

Such men are born leaders of men; but early circumstance drives them within themselves, and out of that inner mortification, from their own slain image, they strive to recreate the world. A visionary poet is a frustrated man of action. The natural poet, a very rare thing, is joyous and therefore the friend of all, the born leader, the truly civilised man. The visionary poet, the philosopher striving that future men shall not suffer in childhood as he suffered, the little brother of Jesus (the man of sorrows and acquainted with grief) writes, out of his enlarged and maimed senses, that children of the future shall be happy: that the sun shall shine on all men equally.

Richard Jefferies, the Wiltshire farmer's son, perceived this; and formulated much of it into words half a century before the World War, by whose glare and shock men began to perceive, beyond the faults of their past lives and education and upbringing and conventions and limitations, the idea of a new world, a natural world, a world wherein men would be happy because of the new wideness of thought arising, phœnix-like, from the mortifying battlefields. Of this world there have been many prophets, whose thought arises into life from faraway centuries and civilisations; and the greatest of them is Jesus of Nazareth. This was the realisation of Richard Jefferies during the last days of his life: the attar of his wisdom.

Thus for the mind of Jefferies.

And of the dying man himself, what can be said? He wrote in his last year, 'Three giants are against me – disease, despair, and poverty.'

> My wearied and exhausted system constantly craves rest. My brain is always asking for rest. I never sleep. I have not slept now for five years properly, always waking, with broken bits of sleep, and restlessness, and in the morning I get up more weary than when I went to bed. Rest, that is what I need. You thought naturally that it was work I needed; but I have been at work, and next time I will tell you all of it. It is not work, it is *rest* for the brain and the nervous system. I have always had a suspicion that it was the ceaseless work that caused me to go wrong at first.
>
> It has taken me a long time to write this letter; it will take you but a few minutes to read it. Had you not sent me to the sea in the spring I do not think that I should have been alive to write it.

An artist friend has described his physical end in words that can hardly be read, by those who love Jefferies' work, without tears.

> It was in the early summer, two or three months before his death, that I saw Jefferies for the last time alive. He had then been living at Goring for some short time, and this was my first visit to him there. I was pleased to find that his house was far pleasanter than the dreary and bleak cottage which he had rented at Crowborough. It had a view of the sea, a warm southern exposure, and a good and interesting garden: in one corner a quaint little arbour, with a pole and vane, and near this centre a genuine old-fashioned draw-well. Poor fellow! Painfully, with short breathing, and supported on one side by Mrs. Jefferies and on the other by myself, he walked round this enclosure, noticing and drawing to our attention all kinds of queer little natural objects and facts. Between the well and the arbour was a heap of rough, loose stones, overgrown by various creeping flowers. This was the home of a common snake, discovered there by Harold, and poor Jefferies stood, supported by us, a yard or so away and

peered into every little cranny and under every leaf with eyes well used to such a search until some tiny gleam, some minute cold glint of light, betrayed the snake. Weakness and pain seemed forgotten for the moment – alas! only for the moment. Uneasily he sat in the little arbour telling me how his disease seemed still to puzzle the doctors; how he felt well able in mind to work, plenty of mental energy, but so weak, *so fearfully weak*, that he could no longer write with his own hand; that his wife was patient and good to help him. He had nobody to come and talk with him of the world of literature and art. Why couldn't I come and settle by? There was plenty to paint. Though Goring itself was one of the ugliest places in the world, there was Arundel, and its noble park, and river, and castle close by. I must go and see it the very next day, and see whether I could not work there, and come back every day and cheer him. I was the best doctor, after all.

Poor fellow! I did not then know or believe that he was so utterly without sympathetic society except his devoted wife. It was so. I am one of the dullest companions in the world; but I had sympathy with his work, and knowledge, too, of his subjects. Well, nothing would do but that I must go to Arundel the next day, and Mrs. Jefferies must show me the town. 'He would do well enough for one day. A good neighbour would come in, and with little Phyllis and the maid he would be safe.'

Therefore we went to Arundel (a short journey by train), and on coming back found him standing against the door-post to welcome us.

I have seldom been more touched than by my experience of that evening, finding, amongst other things, that he had partly planned and insisted on this Arundel trip to get us away so that he might, unrebuked, spend some of his latest hard earnings in a pint of 'Perrier Jouët' for my supper.

Do you know Goring churchyard? It is one of those dreary, over-crowded, dark spots where the once-gravelled paths are green with slimy moss, and it was a horror to poor Jefferies. More than once he repeated the hope that he might not be laid there, and he chose the place where his widow at last left him – amongst the brighter grass and flowers of Broadwater.

He died at Goring at half-past two on Sunday morning, August 14, 1887. His soul was released from a body wasted to a skeleton by six long weary years of illness. For nearly two years he had been too weak to write, and all his delightful work, during that period, was written by his wife from his dictation. Who can picture the torture of these long years to him, denied as he was the strength to walk so much as one hundred yards in the world he loved so well? What hero like this, fighting with Death face to face so long, fearing and knowing, alas! too well, that no struggles could avail, and, worse than all, that his dear ones would be left friendless and penniless. Thus died a man whose name will be first, perhaps for ever, in his own special work.

Foreword to *Richard Jefferies: Selections of his Work, with details of his Life and Circumstance, his Death and Immortality,* edited by Henry Williamson
Faber & Faber, 1937

A First Adventure with Francis Thompson

THOSE who are 'with it', as the current phrase goes, usually have traits of personality in common. Superficially, similar experiences link us with others; but such links seldom hold beyond the limits of shared common experience. Such, for example, is war-time comradeship, when it exists only within the limits of that comradeship. One has only to attend a regimental dinner, when the war is over, to find oneself essentially alone. Faces have changed. We have become sedate, other-worldly, when before we were spontaneous and free. A face may light up at the stir of memory; but like an old film seen again, it has lost something of its pristine impact. Such comings and goings can indeed be nullifying on occasion; anti-climax. That which lives in each memory cannot be shared, save in a moment of time. Then recognition lights the eye, renewing the flow of life: the poetry, or essence, is reshared. Otherwise, behind each changed face a different problem of living keeps us apart.

I 'discovered' the poetry of Francis Thompson in 1917, when I was twenty-one years old. The words stood out from the printed page, making instant impact. They were of the real, or secret world of the spirit of truth behind the outward world of terror and comradeship in which I had my strange and as it were secret existence. It was a world lived for the moment only, against a background of life and death.

I know now, nearly fifty years on – a few tickings of a clock, the passing of days and seasons until, suddenly, all seems to have passed away, while yet it is the same moment in eternity, the same solar orbit round the sun, the same roll of summer stars and, with the coming of the Autumn, Orion glittering low on the southern horizon – I know now that what drew me to Thompson was that we shared the same sense of sight, which with reflection becomes insight; that we were both temperamentally withdrawn from the 'ordinary life' in childhood, sharing the same isolation from our fathers, receiving the same criticism which was the reverse of reassurance (both fathers fearing that their sons would be failures, and suffering disappointment thereby).

A FIRST ADVENTURE WITH FRANCIS THOMPSON

This hiatus in father-affection, accepted, by my unknowing self, as part of ordinary living, caused an imbalance with the mother-image. The condition tended to resistance to maternal love, and to a retreat or secrecy of life in the woods and fields outside my home and giving my love to wild birds and animals.

And then, suddenly, it seemed that the secret life was gone forever, that all had changed in a world of dereliction extending all along the Western Front, from the North Sea to the peaks of the Alps.

This was the only world one knew; and thus, when one first read the verse of Thompson, one's world was identical with that of the poet, who had known the same dereliction, though in the streets of London. There he, too, dreamed of love, which appeared always but to elude him. The lost mother-image – lost because he was no longer a child – was never replaced by the shared love of a woman.

Freud has written that all psychical troubles arise, like poisonous vapour, from repressions of the sexual instinct; and William Blake wrote, a century before, that beauty came from the genitals. Both statements are true symbolically. A balanced life is an harmonious life; we owe both life and harmony to the Creator.

Francis Thompson had deep psychological knowledge, which came from self-knowledge:

> And I deem well why life unshared
> Was ordainèd me of yore.
> In pairing-time, we know, the bird
> Kindles to its deepmost splendour,
>   And the tender
>   Voice is tenderest in its throat:
> Were its love, for ever nigh it,
>   Never by it,
>   It might keep a vernal note,
> The crocean and amethystine
>   In their pristine
>   Lustre linger on its coat.
> Therefore must my song-bower lone be,
>   That my tone be
>   Fresh with dewy pain alway.

So beset, [the poet wrote in his *Shelley* essay] the child fled into the tower of his own soul, and raised the drawbridge. He threw out a reserve, encysted in which he grew to maturity unaffected by the intercourses that modify the maturity of others into the thing we call a man. The encysted child developed until it reached years of virility, until those later Oxford days in which Hogg encountered it; then, bursting at once from its cyst and the university, it swam into a world not illegitimately perplexed by such a whim of the gods. It was, of course, only the completeness and duration of this seclusion – lasting from the gate of boyhood to the threshold of youth – which was peculiar to Shelley. Most poets, probably, like most saints, are prepared for their mission by an initial segregation, as the seed is buried to germinate: before they can utter the oracle of poetry, they must first be divided from the body of men. It is the severed head that makes the seraph . . . And the child appeared no less often in Shelley the philosopher than in Shelley the idler. It is seen in his repellent no less than his amiable weaknesses; in the unteachable folly of a love that made its goal its starting-point, and firmly expected spiritual rest from each new divinity, though it had found none from the divinities antecedent. For we are clear that this was no mere straying of a sensual appetite, but a straying, strange and deplorable, of the spirit; that (contrary to what Coventry Patmore has said) he left a woman not because he was tired of her arms, but because he was tired of her soul. When he found Mary Shelley wanting, he seems to have fallen into the mistake of Wordsworth, who complained in a charming piece of unreasonableness that his wife's love, which had been a fountain, was now only a well:

> Such change, and at the very door
> Of my fond heart, hath made me poor.

Wordsworth probably learned, what Shelley was incapable of learning, that love can never permanently be a fountain. A living poet, in an article which you almost fear to breathe upon lest you should flutter some of the frail pastel-like bloom, has said this thing: 'Love itself has tidal moments, lapses and flows due to the metrical rule of the interior heart.' Elementary reason should proclaim this true. Love is an affection, its display is an emotion: love is in the air, its display is the wind. An affection may be constant; an emotion can be no more constant than the wind can constantly blow. All, therefore, that a man can reasonably ask of his wife is that her love should be indeed a well. A well; but a Bethesda-well, into which from time to time the angel of tenderness descends to trouble the waters for the healing of the beloved. Such a love Shelley's second wife appears unquestionably to have given him. Nay, she was content that he should veer while she remained true; she companioned him intellectually, shared his views, entered into his aspirations, and yet – yet, even at the date of Epipsychidion, the foolish child, her husband, assigned her the part of moon to Emilia Viviani's sun, and lamented that he was barred from final, certain, irreversible happiness by a cold and callous society. Yet, few poets were so mated before, and no poet was so mated afterwards, until Browning stooped and picked up a fair-coined soul that lay rusting in a pool of tears . . .

If, as has chanced to others – as chanced, for example, to Mangan – outcast from home, health and hope, with a charred past and a bleared future, an anchorite without detachment, and self-cloistered without self-sufficingness, deposed from a world which he had not abdicated, pierced with thorns which formed no crown, a poet hopeless of the bays, and a martyr hopeless of the palm, a land cursed against the dews of love, an exile banned and proscribed even from the innocent arms of childhood – he were burning helpless at the stake of his unquenchable heart, then he might have been inconsolable, then might he have cast the gorge at life, then have cowered in the darkening chamber of his being, tapestried with mouldering hopes, and harkened to the winds that swept across the illimitable wastes of death. But no such hapless lot was Shelley's as that of his own contemporaries – Keats, half-chewed in the jaws of London and spit dying on to Italy; De Quincey, who, if he escaped, escaped rent and maimed from those cruel jaws; Coleridge, whom they dully mumbled for the major portion of his life. Shelley had competence, poetry, love; yet he wailed that he could lie down like a tired child and weep away his life of care! Is it ever so with you, sad brother? is it ever so with me? and is there no drinking of pearls except they be dissolved in biting tears? 'Which of us has his desire, or having it, is satisfied?'

It is true that he shared the fate of nearly all the great poets contemporary with him, in being unappreciated. Like them, he suffered from critics who were forever shearing the wild tresses of poetry between rusty rules, who could never see a literary bough project beyond the trim level of its day but they must lop it with a crooked criticism, who kept indomitably planting in the defile of fame the 'established canons' that had been spiked by poet after poet. But we decline to believe that a singer of Shelley's calibre could be seriously grieved by want of vogue. Not that we suppose him to have found consolation in that senseless superstition, 'the applause of posterity'. Posterity, posterity! posterity which goes to Rome, weeps large-sized tears, carves beautiful inscriptions, over the tomb of Keats; and the worm must wriggle her curtsey to it all, since the dead boy, wherever he be, has quite other gear to attend. Never a bone less dry for all the tears!

I have made long quotations from the famous *Shelley* essay, much of it written on used envelopes and other scraps of paper – or the notes for it – while the poet stood at night on the Embankment, in broken boots, under the arch of Waterloo Bridge, where later, in the early years after the Armistice of 1918, I saw workless old soldiers lying on newspapers spread on the paving stones, trying to sleep – no hardship this, after the dreadful crater-zones, filled with water and afloat with corpses in khaki and *feldgrau*, in the morasses below the Passchendaele ridge. Indeed, by comparison of those nights, to sleep on firm stone, out of the rain, was a matter of hugging oneself with secret joy, that one was free, that one was dry, that the long nightmare was over. I have made these quotations (meaning at first to transcribe but a few lines after the poem copied from *Sister Songs*) because of the revelation of how a true poet, sometimes called a major poet, has within his being . . . what today is known as super-sensory perception. He also possesses unusual intuitions. He *knows*. Most people see; but the true poet *sees*. How does he *see*? What links his inner sight with the outward and visible world?

We are all animals, according to modern science – science which, soon after the Passchendaele morasses, was declaring that the 'lower animals' operated solely from instinctive reflex actions. So do, and did we all before and after Pavlov made his discoveries of how animals imprisoned in laboratories behave. But, as Francis of Assisi knew, the birds were blithe spirits of the Creator. In service to one another, two paired birds can do no wrong. They are innocent and loyal, their instincts of loyalty and service to one another are an example to us all. They have not shared the Fall, by which, paradoxically, Man can attain to higher forms of the spirit by way of the Imagination. Are not all forms of life on our planet Creations of the Imagination, hence love, beauty, truth?

> The Church, [wrote Thompson at the beginning of his *Shelley* essay] which was once the mother of poets no less than of saints, during the last two centuries has relinquished to aliens the chief glories of poetry, if the chief glories of holiness she has preserved for her own. The palm and the laurel, Dominic and Dante, sanctity and song, grew together in her soil: she has retained the palm, but foregone the laurel. Poetry in its widest sense (that is to say, taken as the general animating spirit of Fine Arts) and when not professedly irreligious, has been too much and too long either misprised or distrusted; too much and too generally the feeling has been that it is at best superfluous, at worst pernicious, most often dangerous. Once poetry was, as she should be, the lesser sister and helpmate of the

Church; the minister to the mind, as the Church to the soul. But poetry sinned, poetry fell; and, in place of lovingly reclaiming her, Catholicism cast her from the door to follow the feet of her pagan seducer. The separation has been ill for poetry; it has not been well for religion.

Fathers of the Church (we would say), pastors of the Church, pious laics of the Church: you are taking from its walls the panoply of Aquinas; take also from its walls the psaltery of Alighieri. Unroll the precedents of the Church's past; recall to your minds that Francis of Assisi was among the precursors of Dante; that sworn to Poverty he foreswore not Beauty, but discerned through the lamp Beauty the Light God; that he was even more a poet in his miracles than in his melody; that poetry clung round the cowls of his Order. Follow his footsteps; you who have blessings for men, have you no blessing for the birds? Recall to your memory that, in their minor kind, the love poems of Dante shed no less honour on Catholicism than did the great religious poem which is itself pivoted on love; that in singing of Heaven he sang of Beatrice – this supporting angel was still carven on his harp even when he stirred its strings in Paradise. What you theoretically know, vividly realise: that with many the religion of beauty must always be a passion and a power, that it is only evil when divorced from the worship of the Primal Beauty. Poetry is the preacher to men of the earthly as you of the Heavenly Fairness; of that earthy fairness which God has fashioned to his own image and likeness . . .

Eye her not askance if she seldom sing directly of religion: the bird gives glory to God though it sings only of its innocent loves. Suspicion creates its own cause; distrust begets reason for distrust. This beautiful, wild, feline poetry, wild because left to range the wilds, restore to the hearth of your charity, shelter under the rafter of your Faith; discipline her to the sweet restraints of your household, feed her with the meat from your table, soften her with amity of your children; tame her, fondle her, cherish her – you will no longer then need to flee her. Suffer her to wanton, suffer her to play, so she play round the foot of the Cross!

. . . An age that is ceasing to produce child-like children cannot produce a Shelley. For both as poet and man he was essentially a child . . . We, of this self-conscious, incredulous generation, sentimentalise our children, analyse our children, think we are endowed with a special capacity to sympathise and identify ourselves with children; we play at being children. And the result is that we are not more child-like, but our children are less child-like. It is so tiring to stoop to the child, so much easier to lift the child up to you. Know you what it is to be a child? It is to be something very different from the man of today. It is to have a spirit yet streaming from the waters of baptism; it is to believe in love, to believe in loveliness, to believe in belief; it is to be so little that the elves can reach to whisper in your ear; it is to turn pumpkins into coaches, and mice into horses, lowness into loftiness, and nothing into everything, for each child has its fairy godmother in its own soul; it is to live in a nutshell and to count yourself the king of infinite space; it is

> To see a world in a grain of sand,
> And a heaven in a wild flower,
> Hold infinity in the palm of your hand,
> And eternity in an hour;

it is to know not as yet that you are under sentence of life, nor petition that it be commuted into death. When we become conscious in dreaming that we dream, the dream is on the point of breaking; when we become conscious in living that we live, the ill dream is but just beginning.

Coming to Shelley's poetry, we peep over the wild mask of revolutionary metaphysics, and we see the winsome face of the child. Perhaps none of his poems is more purely and typically Shelleian than *The Cloud*, and it is interesting to note how essentially it springs from the faculty of make-believe. The same thing is conspicuous, though less purely conspicuous, throughout his singing; it is the child's faculty of make-believe raised to the *nth* power. He is still at play, save only that his play is such that manhood stops to watch, and his playthings are those which the gods give their children. The universe is his box of toys. He dabbles his fingers in the day-fall. He is gold-dusty with tumbling amidst the stars. He makes bright mischief with the moon. The meteors nuzzle their noses in his hand. He teases into growling the kennelled thunder, and laughs at the shaking of its fiery chain. He dances in and out of the gates of heaven: its floor is littered with his broken fancies. He runs wild over the fields of ether. He chases the rolling world. He gets between the feet of the horses of the sun. He stands in the lap of patient Nature, and twines her loosened tresses after a thousand wilful fashions, to see how she will look nicest in his song . . .

I read this marvellous essay during the late summer of 1917 in Flanders – the wettest summer for forty years – while the field-gun barrages advanced in lines of rolling fire and smoke before the struggling movements of the infantry. Tremendous bubbling thunder filled the very air and made the morass to tremble. Far behind, salvoes from the heavy batteries lining the Menin road east of Ypres droned and grumbled over the watery crater-zones to burst in black villains of smoke upon the concrete German pill-boxes, or massive forts, upon the Frezenberg ridge; beyond which, scarcely perceptible, upon the skyline rose the stump of Passchendaele church, standing nearly five miles east of Ypres and yet barely sixty metres above sea level.

Up there the poor bloody infantry was once again going through it. Rockets of red and green arose above the sultry-speckled bursts of the creeping barrage, 'lifting' twenty-five yards every five minutes to allow the floundering infantry to catch up. Pale golden streaks of fire, as of rain going up instead of down, burst among all the red and green rocket-showers – S.O.S. calls for help from the German *eingreif divisionen* to their batteries on the Gheluvelt plateau on the flank of the advance.

At night we led our pack-mules and horses into the storms of steel and fire descending from the German batteries 'taping' the timber-tracks lying like the sloughed skins of serpents upon the morass glittering with watery shell-holes reflecting the white calcium flares which at twilight began to rise, lilies of the dead, upon the expended effort of the attack.

The salient, a vast negation of darkness, in hopeless travail with the dead weight of human and animal misery, was scored by those white streaks arising in a semi-circle around us: burdened men, charred tree-trunks, sunken tanks were wavery with shadows homeless in the diffused pallor of the night-long flares. To avoid the timber-track, broken and congested by a battalion transport which had just received several direct hits – for these 'corduroy' tracks were under fire from dusk to dawn – I led my string of pack-mules and light draught-horses across the morass, where one fell into a shell-hole nine feet in diameter and seven feet deep at its point of explosion. The driver was killed, the foundering beast snorted and groaned, while water glimmered behind its ears. High explosive shells began to burst all around us, with ruddy glares and rending metallic crashes; bullets, arising in ricochet from the outpost-lines nearer the flares, moaned and piped away overhead with their strange, bird-like pipings. I could hardly move, I stood hot and sweating with half a hundredweight of mud. Somewhere near the voice of a young colonel was cursing in high overwrought screams, for one of the mules had been hurled by a shell amongst his men. They were coming out of the line after relief. As more shells droned down, with their coarse base buzzing descending in scale – the copper driving-band at the base, scored by the gun-barrel rifling made that ominous sound – and screams of wounded horses arose with the cries of men, yellow-forked flames rose to a great height in front, to cast a glare upon the battlefield. They rose up high and narrow, as though the poplars once lining the road were recreated in fire. Some of the tanks going up for tomorrow's attack had been hit by petrol shells. Within a few moments the enemy harassing fire was concentrated on the road where we were to turn off to our dump, and more flaming poplars rose, one beyond the other, into the rainy night. Then a soft downward slurring sound, followed by another and another and another. Plup-plup-plup – gently. Gas shells! My box-respirator, at the alert position across the chest, was a mass of mud. I could hardly discover my face, so heavy and monstrous were my arms. While I was struggling to fit the mask over my nose and lower face, the brutal whine of five-nines swooped down.

Ten hours later about one-third of our mules, their ears drooping – sign of imminent collapse and lying down to die – were standing, mud to fetlocks, along the picket line with its gnawn wooden posts. Some were trying to eat the blankets strapped upon their neighbours. The louring sky – it was, as I have written, the wettest 'summer' in Flanders for forty years – quivered with gun-fire. The infantry were going over again – those who had managed to reach the tape-lines. A minor attack, one of a dozen scarcely mentioned in the official reports during the four and a half months to reach the Passchendaele crest, whence was a view over country held by the enemy for many miles.

After deep sleep within my tent, reading Francis Thompson's 'Peace', while with a pencil I altered, together with few other words, 'Peace' to 'War', thus: (the words in italics my changes) –

> *War:– and* a dawn that flares
> Within the brazier of the barrèd East,
> Kindling the ruinous walls of storm surceased
> To rent and roughened glares,
> After such night when lateral wind and rain
> Torment the to-and-fro perplexed *men*
> With thwart encounter: which of fixture strong,
> Take only strength from the endurèd pain:
> And throat by throat begin
> The *guns* to make adventure of *harsh* din,
> Till all the *mud doth leap in horrid* song:–

One of the poet's night stances – he as it were a sentry posted there –

was in the vegetable market of Covent Garden, among the waggons which brought loads of vegetables along the Old Kent Road, and the broad sett-stoned highway of Whitechapel from the Essex flats. There, some years later, one of the poems of *Sister Songs* recalls his vigil.

> Spring, goddess, is it thou, desirèd long?
> And art thou girded round with this young train? –
> If ever I did do thee ease in song,
> Now of thy grace let me one meed obtain,
>   And list thou to one plain.
>   Oh, keep still in thy train,
> After the years when others therefrom fade,
>   This tiny, well-belovèd maid!
> To whom the gate of my heart's fortalice,
>   With all which in it is,
> And the shy self who doth therein immew him
> 'Gainst what loud leaguerers battailously woo him,
>   I, bribed traitor to him,
>   Set open for one kiss.
>
> *Then suffer, Spring, thy children, that lauds they should upraise*
> *To Sylvia, this Sylvia, her sweet, feat ways;*
>   *Their lovely labours lay away,*
>   *And trick them out in holiday,*
>   *For syllabling to Sylvia;*
> *And that all birds on branches lave their mouths with May,*
>   *To bear with me this burthen,*
>   *For singing to Sylvia.*
>
>   A kiss? for a child's kiss?
>   Aye, goddess, even for this.
> Once, bright Sylviola, in days not far,
> Once – in that nightmare-time which still doth haunt
> My dreams, a grim unbidden visitant –
>   Forlorn, and faint, and stark,
> I had endured through watches of the dark
>   The abashless inquisition of each star,
> Yea, was the outcast mark
>   Of all those heavenly passers' scrutiny;
>   Stood bound and helplessly
> For Time to shoot his barbèd minutes at me;

INDIAN SUMMER NOTEBOOK

Suffered the trampling hoof of every hour
    In night's slow-wheelèd car;
Until the tardy dawn dragged me at length
From under those dread wheels; and, bled of strength,
    I waited the inevitable last.
      Then there came past
A child; like thee, a spring-flower; but a flower
Fallen from the budded coronal of Spring,
And through the city-streets blown withering.
She passed, – O brave, sad, lovingest, tender thing!
And of her own scant pittance did she give,
    That I might eat and live:
Then fled, a swift and trackless fugitive.
    Therefore I kissed in thee
The heart of Childhood, so divine for me;
    And her, through what sore ways,
    And what unchildish days,
Borne from me now, as then, a trackless fugitive.
    Therefore I kissed in thee
    Her, child! and innocency,
And spring, and all things that have gone from me,
    And that shall never be;
All vanished hopes, and all most hopeless bliss,
    Came with thee to my kiss.
And ah! so long myself had strayed afar
From child, and woman, and the boon earth's green,
And all wherewith life's face is fair beseen;
    Journeying its journey bare
Five suns, except of the all-kissing sun
    Unkissed of one;
    Almost I had forgot
    The healing harms,
And whitest witchery, a-lurk in that
Authentic cestus of two girdling arms;
    And I remembered not
    The subtle sanctities which dart
From childish lips' unvalued precious brush
Nor how it makes the sudden lilies push
    Between the loosening fibres of the heart . . .

Eve no gentlier lays her cooling cheek
On the burning brow of the sick earth,

A FIRST ADVENTURE WITH FRANCIS THOMPSON

> Sick with death, and sick with birth,
> Aeon to aeon, in secular fever twirled,
> Than thy shadow soothes this weak
> And distempered being of mine.
> In all I work, my hand includeth thine;
> Thou rushest down in every stream
> Whose passion frets my spirit's deepening gorge;
> Unhood'st mine eyas-heart, and fliest my dream;
> Thou swing'st the hammers of my forge;
> As the innocent moon, that nothing does but shine,
> Moves all the labouring surges of the world.
> Pierce where thou wilt the springing thought in me,
> And there thy pictured countenance lies enfurled,
> As in the cut fern lies the imaged tree.
> This poor song that sings of thee,
> This fragile song, is but a curled
> Shell outgathered from thy sea,
> And murmurous still of its nativity.

This tremendous music continues for page after page, to the glory of love and of life which has its being and all its transformations 'under the fostering hand of the Creator', to employ a phrase used by one in a book composed in prison during the last war, a work* which for its divination and sanctity will one day surely be part of our heritage of literature.

Francis Thompson is a major poet, applauded in his life-time. In the words of his friend and host Wilfrid Meynell, who with his wife, the poet Alice Meynell, cared for him after his days and nights of dereliction in the streets of London, the work of this 'aloof moth of a man' has long suffered the fate of many other great poets, who 'learn in suffering what they teach in song'. His poetry is still 'mighty meat for little guests'. One living minor poet, not so long ago, reviewed a book on the poet's life as 'rags and rubbish', particularly *The Mistress of Vision* which attempts to convey, and does convey, what another living poet, Mr. Robert Graves, calls the White Goddess.

Love is the dayspring of all true poetry, the major force of evolution. There is indeed, as William Blake perceived, a war between Heaven and Hell, of the social instinct which would create higher

---

* The Alternative, by Sir Oswald Mosley

forms of consciousness despite chaos. The imagery of all poetry, as of all religions which strive to create harmony, is a vehicle of this greater love, which arose from within Wilfred Owen – a poet declared, foolishly, by another great poet, Yeats, to be not worth a corner for versifiers in any local newspaper. But even great poets do sometimes disprize their relatives. Did not Byron disesteem the poetry of Keats, until Shelley, the gentle creature, pointed out to Byron his error?

Those charred stumps of trees in High Wood, standing stark on the skyline of the Somme uplands, come to mind as one reads again Thompson's *Hound of Heaven*, to pause, and live again a moment, tenuous and 'unreal' as his *Mistress of Vision*,

> Ah! must –
> Designer infinite! –
> Ah! must Thou char the wood ere Thou canst limn
> with it?

Essay in *The Mistress of Vision*, by Francis Thompson, with a commentary by the Reverend John O'Connor and a preface by Father Vincent McNabb, O.P
Reprinted with an Introduction by Joseph Jerome
Saint Albert's Press, 1966

English Farming

If anyone had told me five years ago that I should be a farmer in Norfolk during the second phase of the Great War, I should not have believed him. Yet my determination to become a farmer, at the age of forty years, was perhaps not so sudden or unpremeditated as at the time I imagined.

Five years ago, in 1936, as I sat by my open hearth in a Devon cottage, while the salmon river outside roared in spate, bringing down roots and trees from the valley which ended as a hillside cut on the wild moor, I realised definitely that I needed new stimulation as an artist. I mused on the orange groves of Florida; the great silver salmon of Newfoundland; the mountains of the Tyrol or the Black Forest, or perhaps Corsica; of the luxuriant forests of New Zealand, with its vision of strange mountains and rainbow trout in the rivers.

I felt I had outlived my Devon countryside, with its otters, foxes, stags, salmon, and badgers. I had written books about these things, also about the village and the people. There was nothing more to write; I had used up all my knowledge.

My four sons were entered for Blundells School; in due course they would go there, and be fitted for some sort of future. What future, I did not know; I had no thoughts, no ideas, about it.

The young men of Britain would have to make their own future. They were Britain; and they would make a new Britain, I hoped, better than the one which I and the friends of my youth had known. We had known what it was to kill, and be killed, about the time we had learned to shave. Afterwards, we walked the streets seeking work; while the Old Men pooh-pooh'd our ideas of a better country. The dole queues remained, and the world did not seem to be getting any better, despite the universal platitudes. Indeed, it seemed to many that the platitudes were a semi-unconscious smokescreen put up to hide reality. A world different from that which broke periodically into war needed fundamental changes; not platitudes.

And so time went on, until five years ago I decided suddenly to do my own small active part in the rebuilding of a better Britain. Farming was in a bad way; so I would start to farm. Many labourers' cottages were rotten; I would rebuild as many as I could. By chance I saw a near-derelict farm in Norfolk, and bought it six months later. I bought it against the advice of lawyers, land valuers, relatives, friends and acquaintances. An experienced farmer told me that English land had not been so cheap for a hundred and fifty years. The near-destitution of so much of the English arable farming was a symptom of the decay of the Old World; but I knew the true English spirit, and believed it was due for a great revival. In that revival, I believed, English land, the mother of the race, and the English people themselves, would be put first.

So I started farming, and in an old lorry took my belongings and part of the family (the others to follow) across England, from the lush West Country, with its rains and rocky streams and soft airs and burring speech, to hardy East Anglia, with its droughts and sluggish rivers and sharp, keen air and shrill, clipped speech. I could not have had such a contrast if I had gone to California or the Rockies – and I was in the best land of all, England!

As I look back now, with the fourth year of my farming venture nearing completion, I am not sorry I turned farmer. People told me I had undertaken a tough job, and I knew it; but I did not know how tough it would turn out. I've had to buy my experience, in everything. Those three condemned cottages, which I rebuilt myself, are finished now; but it took a long time, while farm-work was neglected. When they were done, I had to rebuild and alter two others for a farmhouse; for there was none with the land. The family, five children with father and mother, lived for months in a broken-roofed granary with no windows and a wet brick floor, with only a small stove and no water or bath or drains. The farm was weedy, hedges tall and ragged, gates broken or fallen, the roads were bogs or deep ruts, the buildings ruinous and rat-ridden, the meadows snipe-bogs, the woods full of broken trees and dead elderberries. And all this viewed daily, hourly, by an impatient, imaginative temperament, which longed to see it altered in a moment, but which, to make the transformation real, had to earn money by writing articles, often half the night.

I am glad I undertook the work. Our bullocks lost money (beef didn't pay), the sheep trade fell and flockmasters sold up, wheat was subsidised, and then, at our first harvest, the barley trade (East Anglia grows the finest malting barley) crashed. But I had foreseen a greater decline; and although it meant that my capital was gone and an overdraft was mounting up, I knew things would come right.

They came right when the war broke out. Immediately the Government set about putting things on a proper basis. We farmers now have stable markets. We know what we will get for our pigs, our milk, our sugar-beet, our beef, our mutton. We can plough, cultivate and drill for a crop of barley knowing that we will not only get the bare costs of production back after threshing and taking samples of corn to the merchants at their stands in the Corn Hall, but an increase enabling us to farm better the following season.

My friends and advisers, who thought me rash, even foolhardy, to buy land in 1936, now congratulate me on my foresight. The weeds on the land are gone, the meadows are being drained (Government grant covers half the cost), the arable fields are being chalked (to sweeten the soil, again a half-cost grant), the roads are made up (oh, the blisters of 1937 digging 1,000 tons of flints and gravel out of a pit!), my home-bred bullocks are in the yards, treading clean barley straw to make the dung to grow the corn and the sugar-beet of next season. Sheep graze the grassy hills; the circular saw, driven by the tractor, cuts up tons of firewood from the reclaimed hedges. My three sons go to the village school, while the eldest, aged 14, drives the tractor and ploughs the fields. Their mother looks after the hens, and mends the clothes, while a village maid cleans our small renovated farmhouse and cooks with electricity.

Norfolk is famous for its wild pheasants. Pigeons come from Scandinavia to the woods, and once a week the villagers, by invitation, shoot them from hides in the woods. Wild duck flight to the willow-fringed pond on the meadows, geese pass over, woodcock flap across the North Sea and settle in the hedge-bottoms, trout rise in the chalk stream which runs through the lower land; so we do not lack for food. Our mill in the chaff-barn grinds barley and wheat for flour, for a variety of loaves we bake ourselves. And, of course, we have our own cream and butter. And less this seem too selfish a catalogue, I must add that not the least of our achievements is giving employment to four families and a home to three others in warm, dry cottages. Those four years gave me some white hairs (the placid temperament is best for a farmer's life, with its myriad anxieties!), but I do not regret anything. All was, and is, experience.

INDIAN SUMMER NOTEBOOK

It has taken a war to put British farming on its feet, and to bring back to us generally the idea that work is the true basis of life in the world. A nation that neglects its land, and its peasants – which are its root-stock – will perish. The idea of living by easy money is no good. Napoleon said that toil produced a hard and virile race, while trade produced a soft and crafty people; and that is true. We British are hard and virile, and we must have overseas trade in order to build up a high standard of life; but the cut-price, get-rich-quick idiom was beginning to spoil that hardness and virility. The by-products of that past epoch were over-intellectualism, spiciness and hyper-stimulation of feeling: too many cocktails, too-glamorous movies, a rootlessness showing itself in artistic distortion; pavementism. These things were an emanation of the same system that produced the dole-queues, slums, malnutrition, the 'class-war'. The war has brought us back to the fundamentals of life; and when it is over, on the basis of our new, hard economy, we shall build a fine civilisation in this country, and its Empire, on the simple virtues of life. There will be enough work for everyone under a modernised, planned system which puts first its land and its people.

I want to see town children educated by bodywork in the country, getting to know its trees, its birds, its coasts, its soils, mountains, streams, counties. I want to see country children having technical education; I want to see them travelling to the Empire, and returning with a knowledge of what their inheritance truly means. I want to see thistles and docks as rare plants in Kew Gardens – extinct elsewhere! I desire to see gardens where once there were slums; to see salmon leaping again by London Bridge, in water no longer polluted by sewers, chemical plant, and all the filthy, chaotic dribble of an unplanned, many-headed commercial monster which in the past put profit first and regarded human life as a mere accessory. These and all the other things of a full and proper social life are not only possible, but inevitable; they will arise from the purgatory of the present.

Introduction to *English Farming*, by Sir John Russell
Britain in Pictures series, Collins, 1941

The Winter of 1941

I

ONE day towards the end of October three soldiers on motorcycles arrived by the corn barn of my farm. They were soon followed by an officer in a small camouflaged car. With this obvious advance-guard came several lorries, also camouflaged, and loaded with stores. I regarded them with grim dismay: was I to have another camp on my farm, which meant more scrounging townees stealing hens, eggs, and anything else they could find . . . and of course dumps of filthy litter and young officers regarding me as an old fool whom they (as one once told me) were saving from Hitler? But I tried not to reveal my thoughts when the officer came towards me and without any preliminary whatsoever demanded to know where the water-supply was. I told him, and he turned away, giving an order to a sergeant to bring the water-lorry. I walked after him, and coming to him, said with what easy amiability I could assume, 'Perhaps if you want some water, you will tell me, then I shall ask one of my men to fill your tank for you. Are you passing through the district?'

'We are going to stay several weeks up there,' he replied, pointing to the grassy Home Hills and the woods above.

'Then you are the advance party?'

'That's right,' he replied, obviously wishing to be rid of me. However I was persistent, and said, 'May I see the requisition order? You cannot come here without a requisition order, you know.'

'Haven't you had an order? One has been sent to you.'

'I haven't had it, and until I do receive one, I must ask you not to come here.'

'Well, you can't stop us. There's a war on.'

'Yes, we know; that's why we must safeguard our crops.'

'You'll get compensation.'

'That's not the point. How many are coming?'

'Several hundred, I expect.'

'What's your regiment, please?'

'That I will not tell you.'

'Then what is your name?'

'I'll give you no information.'

He was using the current 'security measure' of giving no information 'likely to be of use to the enemy'. So I thought I would counter that with its equivalent. 'I quite understand; but how do I know who you are? How do I know you are not German parachute troops in British uniform? May I see your identity card, please? I am entitled to ask, you know, as the owner of this land.'

'The captain and the major will be here soon, and I'll send them to you,' he said and turned away.

Perhaps, I thought, he has been primed by the local gossip and black marketeer, who hung about the village Cross and told all and sundry – when they were the sort who would care to listen to such an individual – that I was the local spy and fifth-columnist.

Meanwhile the lorries were moving slowly up the new road we had made with such toil and sweat in the Gulley. They were ten-tonners, and the ribbed tyres tore up the loam-and-gravel surface of the road. At the top of the hill they turned off on the grass, and began to unload their gear by Pine Tree Camp, where I had lived during my first year on the farm. Branches of trees were cut off or torn down for camouflage. After watching this, I went to and asked the officer when the troops were expected. He replied that he wasn't able to tell me. For how long were they coming, I demanded. 'You must ask the officer commanding,' he retorted. I explained that my ewe-flock was on the Home Hills – where they proposed, without authority, to camp – and cows and bull, too, on the only available grass, as the paddock and meadows were flooded after the recent heavy rains. And, being persistent, I asked again about the requisition order.

'You are sure that a requisition order has already been sent to me?'

'That's what I said. Sergeant, move that Bren gun over there.'

'Very good, sir.'

I went home and telephoned the local Anti-Aircraft Gunnery School, which had a permanent camp by the marshes, and learned from the Adjutant that Midland troops were coming to practice for a few weeks, and that their camping site was already allocated on the strip of grass above the marsh known as the Sheep Walk. There would be a lot of them, the voice said, adding, 'I should kick them off, if it were my farm.' I said, 'Thanks, I will,' and seeing the subaltern officer down the road, went after him. Before I could catch him, he went into the public telephone-box. I guessed he was asking for further instructions; and when he came out, I told him that his camping site had been allocated on the Sheep Walk. He made no reply.

Later in the afternoon, an elderly major called with another officer whom he introduced as his second-in-command.

In civil life they had probably been provincial business men, I judged, by their manner and address. The major, who had a heavy reddish indoor face, began by telling me that he had never received a complaint from any farmer on whose land his men had been, and they were coming only for ten days or so, after which another unit was replacing them, and then a third replacing the second lot. I listened, and then asked him straightly:

'Is this land requisitioned, or is it not? If it is, why have I not received the requisitioning order?'

'The order will come, no doubt.'

'But there is doubt, sir, if you will forgive my mentioning it. Will you please give me a direct answer to my question?'

The major looked at the captain. The captain was younger, or looked younger. He wore the two later ribbons of the 1914-18 war, once known as Squeak and Wilfred. The major, whose left breast was modestly vacant of even coronation ribbons, looked like a mayor of some provincial town. He deferred to his junior to deal with this difficult question.

'The order, as far as it is humanly possible to say, is being made out now,' said the captain, suavely, with a smile. I was used to being told lies, which usually I met with a blank and evasive face, except to those nearest to me, when I had tried, with various manners, to convert them to the truth; but nowadays I was tired, and had not the resistance I had before the war; so I continued with toneless persistence,

'I understand that you are supposed to be parking on the Sheep Walk, by the marshes. Your subaltern told me categorically that my land was already requisitioned. Is that a fact?'

'I think he was a little uncertain about his facts,' replied the captain, with an attempt at amiability, adding, 'Of course, you will get compensation.'

'I am not thinking about that, but of my livestock. What area do you intend to occupy?'

'We shall require all the grassland of the hills.'

'What, all the twenty acres of the Home Hills? Will you enter the woods?'

'No, we shall not go into the woods at all. You really need not worry. We have never had a complaint yet.'

'My bull, cows and sheep are already on the twenty acres of grass, the only dry pasture we have. My meadows are flooded, and not only will the grass be trodden into the mud if my stock is put on the meadows, but the ewes' feet will rot and many will die. Your men have left some of our gates open already. If anything happens to the bull or other stock, it will be a serious matter, for which I am legally responsible.'

'Well, we've never had a complaint yet,' repeated the major shortly. I avoided looking at his florid, fleshly face. He looked as though he ate a lot of meat. The lack of medal ribbons was puzzling: surely he could not be younger than myself? But wasn't I looking at this man through the eyes of myself as a soldier a quarter of a century ago? Perhaps he was my junior in years. Heavens, did I look older than that corpulent, that decadent body? What a weary bore I must seem to these two, who probably thought of me as a wretched little farmer concerned with getting all the profit he could out of the war, and now was obstructing troops in their training.

'Well, you see,' I went on, half apologetically, 'I regard my farm as a unit in the home front, to be maintained in full efficiency for the service of the nation, and I assure you that my stock must go on the grass of the hills. Can't you possibly go to your proper camping site which was allocated to you? The adjutant of the Practice Camp told me you were supposed to go on the Sheep Walk.'

The major looked at the captain again.

'We will put sentries on the gates at night,' said the captain. 'I think you will find things will be all right.'

'We've never had a complaint so far,' repeated the major, patiently, smoothly.

'Very well,' I said, after a pause. 'Can I offer you some beer?' They thanked me, but no, they must get back, thanks all the same. I hoped it would not be too bad; and that I had not made myself appear too meticulous. Then, after a hasty meal of bread and cheese and pickled onions, I hurried back to help with the loading of the sugar-beet. It was wet weather, and the beet were thick with mud. Time was precious, time was alarming; soon the frosts might come, and if we did not hurry, the beet might rot in the field. Then there was the ploughing to be done, also before the frost. I hurried up by the Gulley, making myself not look at all the lorries standing on the grass.

Our first sugar-beet returns had shown a 17.3 per cent sugar content; this was for the crop off the Hilly Piece hollow, a poor piece of land when I had come to the farm: since when it had been mucked, dispread with compost, trodden by sheep on roots, marled and ploughed twelve inches deep. We got thirty-six tons of beet off it, and thus paid for all the work in the hollow, as well as making it good for several years.

The next day the rain stopped the sugar-beet lifting. It was heavy rain. We dressed barley in the big barn, putting it through an ancient winnowing dresser I had bought for fourteen shillings just before the war. I dressed the barley for two reasons: to give the men wet-weather work, and to assure myself that the barley was as good as, or better than, the samples by which I had already sold it. Jimmy had put the sheep-folds on the beet-tops, ready for the ewes to go on when the shiny green leaves of the struck-off crowns were wilted. If the 'tops' were fed fresh to sheep, they scoured badly: there was a near-poison in the fresh leaves. Jimmy begged me not to run the ewes on the Home Hills, where now thirty or forty brown-and-black tents and marquees were set up, with half a hundred great six-wheeled lorries drawing Bofors guns. These were parked under the trees. Our new roads were already churned up, and gateposts had been smashed. I had asked the commanding officer not to use the lower road – thus avoiding the Gulley – but to enter and go out by the top road, which was already spoiled by the lorries of the permanent searchlight camp on Twenty-One Acres. He said he would do all he could to help me, but all his help was nil, for the lorries used the lower road, coming down off the grass which they had deeply rutted and churned, bringing soil on the tyre-patterns to the road, and adding to the liquid mud already lying in the pot-holes they had torn. Rain fell every day; and soon the roads were worse than they had been the first winter I had viewed the derelict farm, before the war. I asked for an order limiting the speed of the monsters to 5 m.p.h., but they roared to and fro as before. The loamy gravel we had dug and spread so laboriously four years before – nearly a thousand tons of it in under two months – was scattered; the grass was churned to blackness; branches of trees everywhere torn down; doors lifted off iron hooks from stable and granary, to be used as washing perches beside the river; the tool kit of the Silver Eagle, which stood in a bay of the hovel, stolen, with a new alarm clock for which I had waited ten months, together with a pair of shoes left in the back under the tonneau cover. Sacks went from the barn, and other tools from the workshop were missing.

Jimmy said the ewes would take fright easily, and slip their embryonic lambs, if something were not done. We were compelled to have them lie on the paddock, which was swampy. Many were limping; we had pared their feet, treated the rot with ointment, but the wet was fatal. Tom the Aberdeen-Angus bull and his cows had to remain on the Home Meadow, although it should have been closed to all stock now, since it was under water. What had been a green and level sward was now a mess of deep watery hoof-holes. And still no requisition order had been served upon me.

On the last day of October I helped to sack up, in the corn barn, one hundred and six coombe of our Hilly Piece barley, and then we began to lift the two-hundred-weight sacks onto lorries taking the load to Whelk Station. The next day I stayed in bed, watching the rain flawing the window-panes; I felt giddy and cold, despite the electric fire; but work had to be done, so I got up in the afternoon and went to Whelk Station to collect sacks for the next day's wet-weather sacking-up of the next lot of barley. Without sacks there could be no sacking-up, no wet-weather work for the men. When I came back I heard that the owner of the Old Castle – who had come to the village the same year as ourselves and had spent four thousand pounds on putting the Elizabethan house in order – had fallen at the top of his drive, as he was going for a walk. He was dead when they picked him up. He was a kind, gentle, aloof man, seeming always so tired and lonely. He had come to the little valley to find peace; and now, surely, he had found it, I thought, as I lay in bed that evening with a temperature of one hundred and three and a burning throat.

The early days of November were cold and murky. After two days of fretting in bed, I got up and walked round the farm, feeling myself to be the ghost of my former living. I hurried past the wretched swedes and mangolds of the Lower Hanger – scarcely bigger than cricket balls – which the men were lifting, to the wheat on the Higher Hanger which looked well up. I was glad I had persisted in my own way and got it in early. Dick and Norman were thatching the meadow-hay stack on the causeway between the Home and the

Camping Hill meadows. The bitumenised paper laid on the stack by the cartshed in June was already rotten. So much for the advertisements in the farming journals!

When I came to the haystack by the Duck Decoy, I saw a wretched sight. Soldiers had clambered upon it, leaving broken depressions in the thatched roof. The heavy rains had drained into the holes made by foot and knee; the stack must either be re-thatched – and we were already far behind with our work – otherwise the rains would rot the heart of it. I found two men sitting there, enjoying the view; two friends, maybe, with boyhood memories of a world which had a horizon for them. I had not the heart to ask them to get down. My throat was still bad, and hurt me to speak and swallow; I hurried on, to look at the bow-backed and limping sheep.

The roads were chains of lagoons. More gateposts were bashed into and cracked off, to lie splintered or pushed askew. In my low state – actively girding against the war and all that the war was, both effect and cause, in the human beings about me – the condition of the farm seemed to be symbolic of the condition of urbanised mankind. The ruined roads, costing so much in ceaseless work in the past, were a symbol of the vanity of hope and constructive endeavour. Was it for this – to be arrested and imprisoned without charge or trial, as a suspected traitor – that one had gone through the Somme and Passchendaele? For this, that one had striven to clarify the mind, to see, and then to tell in words, the truth? Life without honour was mere existence; it was more honourable to be dead. Cold and hollow, set in a wasting scorn and despair, I returned to bed, but could not rest: I must work: I must write of things I had known before they were lost in death's dateless night. Reaching for my diary, I found I could only record the bare outline of facts. Nine ewes had died on the swampy paddock in one week. For several days they had been feeding on their knees, to avoid the pain in their fevered feet; they had ceased to feed, had lain down, and died, having lost heart.

There were no oats for the horses, since the threshing contractor had deliberately broken his word about coming to thresh our only oat-stack, on which we depended for food for all our horned stock and also the ewes near lambing time. The oat-stack was built beside the Duck Decoy, and the way to it was now impassable, being low-lying and soggy. The horses were doing heavy work, carting the sugar-beet off Fourteen Acres. Even if the threshing tackle arrived, it would find the approach to the oat-stack impassable, with its fifteen-ton engine, until March or April. And oats were not to be bought during that winter of dearth and food shortage.

One morning as I watched over thin beasts moodily eating chaffed barley straw and sugar-beet pulp, Robert, my small son, approached with a sidebag of breakfast for me, and with the mail. There was a letter from the District Claims Office, which I read as I swallowed a toast-and-bacon sandwich.

'With reference to your telephone call of yesterday, I have been in touch with the Sub-Area Quartering Commandant and he was unaware that any part of your farm was in use by Military Personnel and steps are being taken immediately to enquire into the circumstances of this occupation, and to regularise the matter by formal requisition if he is satisfied the occupation warrants such action.'

Perhaps, I thought, the enquiry might result in the farm being taken over as a permanent practice area. Some of the big lorries had got as far as the Hanger yard; over the layer of Hilly Piece; on Spong Breck: despite the aldermanic major's assurance that only the hilly grassland would be occupied.

I had to return to bed, as my temperature rose again; I had what was called a septic throat, and would not see a doctor. My son was most patient with me at this time, a boy of fifteen standing silent and unresponsive at the bottom of the bed. I told him I did not mind what he did, if he would always come to me straightly, and report any accident or error, without untruth: that it was a rare thing among men first to be able to see the truth, and then to learn how to utter or tell it. I know it was a sign of ineffectuality in myself as a parent to talk like that; but only words seemed left to my life.

I read in the newspaper that Lt.-Col. Sir Arnold Wilson, C.M.G., D.S.O., M.P., who before the war had striven for clarity between Germany and Britain and Italy, and thereby had been much criticised by his inferiors, had, when the war had broken out, joined the R.A.F., qualified as a rear-gunner in a bomber and had fallen in flames in the summer of 1940, aged fifty-six. In the mood of frustration that bound my life at this period, it seemed more and more true that honour existed only among the dead and those about to die, and in those in prison without trial.

A letter the next day from the merchants who bought the one hundred and six coombe of barley said it arrived at their maltster's wet, and they asked me to say that it was in good condition before leaving the farm. I was happy to reply that it had left in first-class condition.

I was out and about, hesitantly, on Thursday the 22nd November, and on Saturday I went to Norwich market. There I learned that barley, the one cereal that was not controlled, was now 84s. a coombe for fine; 75s. for medium; 70s. for common or tail. I had bought my next year's seed at the end of October for 70s., once-grown pedigree Archer-Spratt, and wondered immediately afterwards if I had been silly; but I had an idea that the price would go up, and had acted on it, though somewhat trepidantly. When I had seen an acquaintance a few minutes later, at another stand, and had asked him if it were advisable to buy seed then, he had replied that he wouldn't; that the price then ruling would not last, when more barley came into the market. He was a member of a famous local firm of barley merchants. Perhaps it was policy to say this, lest farmers held back their grain for the price to rise, as now it had risen.

I went to London, for a change, and stayed a night at the Barbarian Club, or what was left of it after the blitz. The Club was very short of staff, also of food. An old fellow with a purple face in the bar and without the slightest provocation from me, shook his fist in my face, spluttered about his grandsons at Dunkirk, and said I ought to be in prison. I returned from London, feeling the usual negation which began at Liverpool Street, and increased all the way through the massed and bomb-broken houses of the East End to Whelk-next-the-Sea, where I alighted in darkness, and void of personality. Gradually the farmhouse parlour, with its whitewashed walls, chestnut beam across the ceiling where horse brasses and pewter mugs hung, its walnut cupboard and gate-leg table, armchairs and rush-mats on the red tiled floor and tea laid on the long polished refectory table, ruddy fire of bull-thorns in the open hearth, all the children to greet me, a tidy and nice room, and Loetitia always kind and ready to smile, annulled much of the negation of the world, wherein Britain seemed to be dying. I was told that the troops had left the farm, and the District Claims Office had rung up, with a view to coming out from Norwich to see me shortly, by appointment.

II

Before the visit of the Claims Officer, I went round with a notebook to write down the details of my claim. The lower road was still a chain of muddy lagoons. The granary door had floated down the river. The horse-trough was full of soapy water. Many more gateposts were smashed. The Gulley road was impassable, being a foot deep in mud. The sand pit, whence the best sand in the district for building was sometimes taken, was filled in; underneath lay broken bottles and tins and garbage. The undergrowth in the woods was trodden, branches of trees had been torn and chopped off for firewood. Apparently soldiers of the modern army disliked to use latrines as much as they did in my war; when on the Somme battlefield every shell-crater in summer had its little relic of private meditation. The woods were foul to walk in. The wire fences were trodden down. Hen houses had been smashed for firing. Altogether fourteen ewes had died in the swampy paddock. Nearly all the hens had disappeared. Scores of small iron screw-pickets, used for tents, remained in the grass at the wood's edge. Obviously no officer had been detailed to look round before departure. Windles said he had seen soldiers in the workshop, handling my tools. Bits of paper and empty tins lay everywhere on the hills. Sacks had been taken, and straw. The commanding officer had left with his illusions unshattered – there had been no complaints.

A subaltern of the Claims Department came out by car, to look around with me. He was an affable fellow. In the back of the camouflaged military car lay a .410 gun. He asked me who had the shooting. I said I had the shooting. With a laugh, he left the .410 gun in the back of the car.

'This is too much for me to deal with,' he said, when we had gone round. 'I think I'll tell the Big Chief.'

The Big Chief came three days later, by appointment. My throat was bad again, and I got out of bed, with deep reluctance, ten minutes before he was due to arrive. The Big Chief certainly was a big man, as size went. As he walked in a stately manner up the pavor'd path, I saw, through the lattice window, that he was tall, and in a manner impressive, with red face, supercilious expression, distant eyes, and long nose. I opened the door for him, and said How do you do; he came in, bending under the arch, and without any reply put his hat and leather-covered cane on the table. He wore the ribbons of two coronations and his highly-polished field-boots and cane and uniform all looked to be from the last war; or maybe from Moss Bros. Slowly he removed his dogskin gloves, tossing them negligently into his hat on the table. I almost expected him to start whistling, for his mode or manner was reminiscent of a Jewish-Australian comedian called Albert Whelan whom I had seen as a boy, a comedian who always appeared in evening clothes and top-hat, and whistling melodiously. But instead of a liquid whistle, the Big Chief turned abruptly to me and said curtly, 'Now for your case! Have you a claim made out?'

'No, I haven't made one yet.'

'Then you make no claim?'

'Yes, I do. Of course I do.'

'For what amount?'

'I hardly know. I – '

'Now I've looked round the roads. The material, I cannot call it metalling, appears to be unsuitable for traffic, your own included.' He looked at me accusingly.

'It was the best we could get in 1937, when we made up all the roads which are now ruined.'

'You talk of ruined roads, but let me tell you this, if Hitler came wouldn't he do a great deal more damage, and what sort of claim would he consider from you? And after all, these fellows are defending your life for you, you know! And here's another point: under Defence Regulation Fifty-two, the competent military authority, any troops, that is, can enter any land or building at any time, and you have no power to stop them. Therefore your point about the absence of a requisition order, made in your letter to my office, does not arise. Have you anything to say?'

The feeling of being hopelessly in the wrong about everything came over me: I could say nothing.

'Now we'll look round together,' he went on, in a changed tone of voice, with a trace of friendliness in it. 'Of course it looks worse than it really is. When the dry weather comes, you'll hardly notice the mud. It will turn to dust, and blow away! However, we will certainly allow you something for the pot-holes.'

He took up gloves, cane, hat; and I followed him out.

The Big Chief's soldier-servant-chauffeur was waiting by an old suburban saloon car, carefully cleaned. I got in after the Chief. We drove to the lower road. The car swayed slowly, splashing through the chain of lagoons. Its springs were set, i.e. tired and flat, and the body took the bumps almost direct. Then we came to the area of dark mud, lying several inches above the disrupted surface, where the turf of the verges had been churned with water and gravel. The driver changed to bottom gear. Thereafter the road rose, and there was no water. Leaving the car by the barn, we got out. I followed the officer up the Gulley. I followed him down again.

'No, it isn't so bad as it appears,' he remarked casually. 'Now we'll take these roads in sections. Up the hill here, what do you consider a fair price for removing the mud? There are about 250 yards. A day's work for a man? Eight bob?'

'Two days, at least. But we haven't the labour. We are behind with the sugar-beet.'

'Everywhere is the problem of labour, my dear sir, thanks to those swine in Hunland.'

'Can you get the Garrison Engineers to make these roads up?'

The Big Chief shook his red face, twice; and I understood that the matter was dismissed.

'Very well, we'll say two days' labour. Now how many yards for dressing the surface of this stretch. We'll call it No. 1 stretch. Two yards?'

Two cubic yards of gravel weighed about two and a half tons. I tried to calculate. Two hundred and fifty yards long, multiplied by 3 yards, made 750 square yards. Gravel two inches thick was one-eighteenth of a yard deep. Divide 750 by 18: I worked this out on an envelope and said:

'It will require forty cubic yards at least to make it as it was before.'

The Big Chief cut the air with his short cane; tapped his long and polished riding-boot; projected his entire personality upon me in a direct stare. I felt that an enormous turkey was leaning down to peck me. 'Now let me tell you this! The payment is *ex gratia*; you can accept it or leave it. I happen to be a chartered surveyor, and I say that five yards will restore this road to its pristine condition. Five yards, say at 7s. 6d. a yard. Right.' He made a note of it.

'What about these ruts on the grass? One day's digging by one man should rectify them. Well?'

'Two days.'

The Chief raised the skin of where his eyebrows had once been.

Perhaps I could plough the ruts level. Cultivate the churned waste. The grass anyway was old and tired, it was congested. It would do it good.

'Very well, two days.'

'Next item.'

'Broken wire under that wood.'

I followed the Big Chief there. He did not appear to walk; he stalked there. Pink flesh bulged out of his collar.

'H'm, pretty rotten wire. Rusted away. How do I know it wasn't broken before they came?'

I ignored his remark and said, 'Can't I claim replacement value?'

'Very well. Replacement value. I have a roll of rusty wire, and it shall be delivered to you. Next please.'

'Who's going to erect it?'

'You are. We've all got to make sacrifices in this war.' The Big Chief said this while making a note. 'Next.'

'The trees in the wood are torn about, some cut down.'

The Big Chief shook his head. 'Next.'

'My sand pit is filled in, and is but a trash heap now. Valuable, perhaps, as an item of agenda for the Society of Archaeologists in five centuries time, with its broken crockery and rusty corkscrew pickets; but for me, it spoils the building sand. It was a good pit and was in order before they camped here.'

The Big Chief cocked a glance at me. 'How often do you take sand?'

'Whenever we need it.'

'H'm. Half a crown to dig it out. Next.' It had taken Norman and myself an entire day to clear it a few months before.

'This broken gatepost.'

'It's rotten at the base. Look – dry-rot. Next.'

'It was struck by a fifteen-ton lorry.'

The Big Chief shook his head. 'It's had its day. Quite rotten. Next.'

'It should be replaced. My gate was all right before the troops came.'

'Now we'll take this road up here.'

'No, that's to be done by another unit, on this requisitioned site.'

'Right. Down the hill.'

We descended.

'Now for these pot-holes. No. 2 stretch. A dozen yards should fill them. Three days to clear the mud. That's what I'll allow you. It's quite fair.'

'It won't restore the road as it was.'

'What farm road is ever anything but pot-holes and muck?'

'I wrote a book about this farm, and there are two photographs in it, of Before, and After. I'll show you when we get back to the cottage. We spent several hundred pounds making this lower road, and the top road.'

'H'm. Twelve yards, at 7s. 6d. a yard. Thirty bob for scraping mud. It's quite fair. Next.'

'Very well, but it won't be enough. I know what I'm talking about. I made the roads. I did the digging and spreading, and the paying.'

'And I know what I'm talking about, my dear sir. I've made hundreds of roads. And I do the surveying and the costing. Next.'

We went to the granary. The missing door-space was pointed out.

'How do I know there was a door there?'

'I really cannot add to what I have said.'

The Big Chief grunted. The landscape looked colourless, drab, untidy, meagre, decadent.

'I have a witness,' I said, a little sorry for having snubbed him.

'H'm. Very well, say five bob?'

'Very well.'

'Next.'

'The road up to the higher fields.'

The Big Chief looked bored. A picture of Windles' cockerel, Hawkeye, fighting the turkeys two winters before, came into my mind. The Big Chief walked with the deliberation of a turkey; he had the dignity of a turkey as it peers forward, cautiously, quietly, to give a sudden peck at a smaller hen. That was why Hawkeye fought sixty damned gobblers, Hawkeye protecting his hens, attacking against great odds as he ran forward, only to retreat before the invading semi-circle of gobblers, stalking forward, heads ready to strike, heads knowing no mercy. It was always a losing fight for Hawkeye, mongrel smoke-grey and white cockerel, but always Hawkeye fought. The Big Chief looked much like a gobbler, his pendulous cheeks taking on a bluish tinge in the cold damp air by the river.

'I don't want to see the road up there,' he said. 'How long is it?'

'Two fifty yards.'

THE WINTER OF 1941

'Say the same as No. 1 Stretch. Anything more?'
'Ruts over the clover layer.'
'Roll them out. Won't hurt your layer. Next.'
'Fourteen ewes died in the swamps.'
The Big Chief shook his bluish chaps. 'No proof, may have had fluke. By the river. Next.'
'The Home Meadow is badly poached. I don't mean by poachers. By cattle left on it, owing to troops on the hill grass. We rolled it last spring, and harrowed it.'
'It won't hurt it to roll it again. No claim for that. Nothing more?'
'I don't think so.'

I was numb I didn't care, it was all part of the condition of war in people's minds and little selfish egos. Once I saw a partridge chick, no bigger than a bumblebee, run near a turkey which leaned down and struck it dead. Just that; and left it feebly twitching. We walked back to the car. There was a little mud on the Big Chief's boot-heels. With leisurely indifference he put one foot on the fender of his car, and beckoned his driver. The driver hurried up with a cloth, and wiped off the heel. Then, with the same leisurely indifference, he removed the foot and put up the other foot. That too was cleaned. The Big Chief, giving neither glance nor word to the driver, then removed the foot.

The lofty manner was very slightly relaxed over a glass of beer in the parlour, while he made out the claims and I signed them. Then I asked him when he thought the war would be over.

He looked at me deliberately with his calculating pale eyes aslant and said distinctly, 'When we've ground those pigs into the mud!'; and taking up gloves, cap, and stick, he called out 'Good day!' and returned along the pavored way as he had come.

Perhaps as one concerned with the saving of public money, the Big Chief did his job well, perhaps too well; for I heard later that there were many complaints of how he dealt with farmers' claims; and later still, that he had been promoted, and sent to another command. I learned also that his job before the war had been the selling of little houses of a Housing Estate on the hire purchase system, with weekly payments extending over a quarter of a century or so. I expect he was a good salesman. It was no doubt a weakness in me that did not allow me to stand up to him with his own manner and attitude, or to see the comic side of the affair; I remember that his remark about pigs

INDIAN SUMMER NOTEBOOK

being ground into the mud hurt me deeply, perhaps because in my youth I had seen so many dead men, and wounded men not yet dead, lying in mud during and after battles, and also my isolation in a district where I was unpopular, and the weakness caused in part by a septic throat made me unduly sensitive: for when he had gone, I recall that I wept, thinking of men drowning in water and burning in the air, or lying in the searing desert sands and the icy steppes of Russia; and such was my illusion, I believed that the ruined condition of the roads and that of the Western world were one and the same thing; and I could not do anything about it any more.

Contribution to *The Pleasure Ground: A Miscellany*
of English Writing,
edited by Malcom Elwin
Macdonald, 1947

Indian Summer Notebook

1

MY SPIDER, MY BEE

During the last thirteen years I nearly wrote myself to perdition. By day and by night I sat within my hilltop hut in Devon, anti-social and convoluted, spinning webs of words.

Outside in an alien world the sun curved a little higher in its daily arc, the summer stars shone, the planet Mars glowed dull red above the southern horizon. Then the sun's curves were descending and Sirius the Dogstar, following Orion the Hunter, was baying his green fires below the glittering constellations of winter.

The grass was frosty, cold winds drove salt-spume on my western window. Somehow it was the spring equinox, and tractors were in the fields harrowing-in barley. Upon my open hearth a beechwood fire had burned for months, years on end, never going out. A copper oil-lamp, table, couch with shepherd's plaids – my comforters, my security from the flare-haunted nights of First Ypres, green-slanting shadows of trees, crack of sniper's bullet, brutal downward dronings of Jack Johnsons, the five-nines of the Alleyman.

Dare one open the door in those winter nights come again? Stars hung above the beech spinney, Northern Crown and Great Bear, faithful Polaris. Meteors slid in lines of pale fire, distant roar of waves upon the sands of Croyde and Saunton, beating on the rocks of Baggy headland. The world-rimming lighthouse-flashings of Harty Point and Lundy. Tremendous exhilaration! For thirty years I had waited to write my novels of Ypres, Somme, Seigfried Stellung . . .

The harder I worked – 10, 12, 15 hours on stretch – the greater the feeling of freedom in achievement. When I could see no more I sank, with stinging eyes, fully dressed upon the couch, to awake with a glow both rich and strange, that all was balanced in Time.

'Does this mean that you will never write again about nature?' someone asked on a sunny spring morning. 'What, you haven't been round Baggy for years? Or crossed the Burrows? Exmoor? Walked by Salar's river?'

My body was growing old. My spirit growing young again, and

fresh. My eyes were lost without spectacles. 'No time ever again, to stand and stare?'

No time. November gales in the valley of the Ancre. A force-9 wind threw five beech trees in the spinney. When they were sawn I counted 110 rings, each a tree-year. I split and stacked the logs myself and when all had been turned to potash on the hearth the five 1914-18 novels were done. The author lost, vacant, aimless. In T.E. Lawrence's words about himself, in a letter written just before he died, 'the mainspring seems broken'. One must work on, through another war and so to my climax. Fifteen volumes to the end.

It is summer again. Thousands of people on the sands. Transistors, cars glittering. To Baggy headland? By the path along North Side someone had tipped tons of domestic and other rubbish in that quarry where the kestrel used to nest, and blue borage flowers once grew. Turn back. I am old, I am *ancien régime*. I must clean my salt-crusted, smoke-oily, web-laden windows. A pail of water. Already half-filled. O, a dead bumble bee. Poor innocent honey-spinner, flower-maker. Why did I go to sleep in the grass, leaving the pail half-full? When I have so much work to do.

I poured away the water. The bee lay in the sun. Verdict: Found drowned. Stay, was that a hooky black leg stirring? Run for blotting paper. It lives! In the heat of the sun, upon my palm, crawling feebly.

What of its young in nest down a hole somewhere in the mossy bank, waiting for this faithful Queen Victoria? I had honey in a jar. Run. Old honey, jar almost empty. Fermented. No matter.

Bee back on palm, dry, lancing long black tongue tipped brown, sip, sip, sip, 100 sips to the minute, tiny tiptaps on my skin. Filling itself with fuel. Another drop. Sip, sip. Filling reserve tank before taking off? Wings and head cleaned. Taking off. Oh dear, crash landing after Immelmann turns, half rolls, zoom and stall. Verdict: Drunk in charge of aircraft.

Try again. My bee flew up, she went zig, she went zag, and clung to my hair. I bore her thus to my hut to sleep it off, away from enemy birds, mice, snakes in the grass. I left her on the window sill.

So I come to my spider. A black horror. A junk-shop ghoul. Empress Arachne of Darkness. Frowsty flattish web clotted with wreckage of bluebottles, moths, daddylonglegs, butterflies. Eight spiky legs, battery of eyes, bull's-horn pincers and the speed of a dragster.

INDIAN SUMMER NOTEBOOK

Buzz of entangled wings made her rip out of her tunnel tearing threads, back again dragging prey poisoned by those hollow mandibles. A score of times I had meant to sweep away her charnel house, but I let live.

Back to my bee. She was sleeping it off. Now to clean the windows outside. Pail of water from across the field. When I returned by, bee was buzzing in the web. I stood by to help: Nemesis.

Empress Arachne came out of her tunnel. She waited, moved forward. Watched Queen Bumble. Other bee-shucks littered the web. But she didn't advance. I stood and stared, feeling her hesitancy. She ran back. Had she seen the glistering eye of Nemesis?

No need for force. Queen Bumble crawled along a known finger. Put on silver birch tree outside in the sun. And wandering lost in the tiny apple-orchard called the Lozenge, I scooped a warble fly from a wasp-hollowed apple. Warble was tanglilegs, as they used to say in Devon. On cider. I dislike warble flies, drunk or sober. They blow eggs on bullocks' legs, maggots bore in, tunnel their way to the spine, and pupate just under the skin. Thence they tunnel out in due season and spread wings to mate and blow more eggs.

So into the web of the Black Widow went Warble the Leather Spoiler, while I justified a return of guilty small-boy torture feelings for the sake of the Boot and Shoe Industry.

Empress Arachne ran forward. Again she stopped about two inches off the intruder. Went back. *Why* was she hesitant? I put fly after fly into her web, she never touched them, all escaped by way of my finger. The Black Empress seemed to have lost her nature. So gentle, so inoffensive. I put on my spectacles, and all was clear.

In one corner of the web was a burst ball of silk. This was the climax of her life. All lust, all passion spent. What force had transformed this tiger, tiger burning bright, in the forests of the night, into a Blakeian saint? Day after day I stood and stared, as she withered away, face turned to the wall, while from the burst ball of silk tiny spiders were moving to spin out their own lives.

2
LEAVES IN THE GRASS

I sit in the sun outside my hut, and watch a lizard sunning itself on one of the elmboards, near a knothole, its home. I am lamenting my vanished partridges.

Years ago a pair always nested in this field, season after season. And a white owl quartered the mice-runs in the grasses. Were they gone with the quails which had haunted ventriloquially this nature reserve of neglected pasture now tumbled down to what farmers call rubbish – docks, knapweed, dandelions, hawkweed (those blazing little suns) and delicate pink fumitory?

Wet-my-lips is the haunting sunset and moonlight cry of the quail, small bird of the partridge family which migrates in spring from the burning deserts of North Africa, once littered by the wreckage of 8th Army and Afrika Korps. A cry that haunts . . .

Quail and partridge, white owl drifting moth-like over the mice-runs, where were they? Died out, with so many other birds in this age of science which knows so much, and yet so little?

The diesel fumes of tractor and lorry fill the air about me, overlaying the scents of flowers. At my apple-blossom the bee sucks no more. Ariel, too, is gone, and the lyric girdle of the earth, my world. Money bounces messages off Telstars, and, when the wind is still, a layer of industrial smog from the Midlands lies over Exmoor. Another stratifies over the channel. I have seen it from a glider, level black band between earth and azure. My son John, who sometimes pilots me aloft, says it comes from Paris, and industrial Northern France.

I believe that the purpose of life on this earth is to create beauty. The lyric did not die on the Somme, with many of the Georgian poets, as once I thought. Nor did it die in Russia. There was Pasternak, now there is Paustovsky. So close down waste-land thoughts. Shut up, Williamson, and get on with your story of the beech leaves in the grass. Down there, by your feet. A yard away, to be exact. A small cluster of dry brown leaves, smaller than the outline of a man's cap.

I am sitting outside my hut. The windows are clean, my bee (you may remember I left her on the silver birch bark) has found her nest. I followed her hang-over flight to a clump of cock's-foot grass near the Lozenge. She's safe. Watched by a lizard, I sit idling, clad only in shorts and shoes, while sunlight converts my writing-table fat into food. And vaguely I am wondering about that little heap of last year's beech leaves, curled dry and brown, in the young green grasses by the path I cut through my acre of weedy rubbish, or nature's reserve.

Ah! I am being watched by more than a lizard's eyes. That cautious *gock* coming from somewhere in the longer grasses. I recognise it happily, the sentinel call of a male partridge. So there *is* a pair in the field, after all.

Slowly, slowly, inch by inch, put on long-distance spectacles. Then raise head gradually while keeping eyes closed. Open them *dully*. There he is, head erect, on an anthill. On guard.

It is half an hour after noon. It is the time a cock partridge calls his hen, after prolonged scanning of sky, to feed. Twenty minutes for lunch, then she must return to her nest. That *gock* means, Do not come yet.

The sky is clear of crow and hawk, so it must be that I'm in the way. So, slowly into the hut. Keep well back from the eastern window.

Brown jersey on for camouflage. Take a look at Pertris through the Zeiss monocular glass . . . yes, his head is lower: those egg-thieves, those tree-top watchers the crows, whose eyes are as keen as his and as knowledgeable, are not in the beech spinney.

It is cold waiting in the hut. My trees, planted in 1930 when I built the hut, have grown tall. All late spring and summer the hut lies within a dark green shade. One needs a fire there when writing, even on a hot day, for the act of imaginative creation draws strength from the body: cold sweats accompany the flow of images being turned into word symbols.

I turn to the spider, the Empress Arachne. I think of Lenin's prophecy that the State, when all shall have been achieved, will wither away. The Empress Arachne's race is run. She has fulfilled herself. Scores of tiny, semi-transparent spiders, her children, have inherited her realm.

The cock partridge isn't to be seen. The hen has probably joined him. It is cold in the hut.

I sit outside in the sun, its benison oozing into my veins, and I see that the beech leaves in the grass have gone. In their place are

INDIAN SUMMER NOTEBOOK

fragments of *sycamore* leaves. But sycamore leaves are not like the leaves of the beech, which are pushed off by new breaking buds in spring. Sycamore leaves fall in the autumn, each with its black patch of decay, and soon disintegrate in winter rains. Those are not leaves. *Those* are the dark brown back-feathers of a hen partridge. So she crept back while I was in the hut and covered the beech leaves with her body; and then, slowly bending her neck in a series of slow movements, had withdrawn one after another of those beech leaves with which she had camouflaged her eggs.

I watched her, again from the window, making little piles of them, like plates for removal from a table. (Later, when her eggs hatched, she made neat piles of the half-shells, to conceal them while her chicks dried off under her, before she led them to cover in the long grasses.)

For many days, coming and going down the path, my feet must have passed within inches of her as she squatted there, never moving. Partridges sit tight. Many a hen has been decapitated, body still covering the eggs, before the knives of a mowing machine.

At four o'clock Pertris was once again watching from his anthill. From the narrow window in the loft of the hut I watched the hen taking brown leaf after brown leaf to tuck them between and over her dozen or so olive-brown eggs, before creeping off to her sentinel lover. A tortoise creeping through the grass.

And suddenly a screaking cry, and from the middle of the field both birds exploded up noisily, thus to attract attention away from the nest, should any paw'd or wing'd predator be on the prowl. My partridges glided over the hedge into the next field, there to feed on insects and to pluck seeds from grasses gently astir in a susurrating wind coming inland from the sea.

3

BLUE HALLS OF THE WIND

It was one of those mornings when one feels glad to be alive. I wonder if it is generally known how atmospheric variations affect human life, as well as animal life, which includes fish and insects? Look at those clouds of cirrus cumulus, dissolving as one glances into the blue sky, while feeling the heart lifting, seeing the colours of tree, grass, flower and bird to be visibly increasing.

Down in the valley stream I know the waterflies are swimming up as nymphs, to split their pellicles and rise as winged creatures into what must be for them a paradise. Their mouths are sealed, they will need neither food nor drink; their year of underwater life is over, now all is for love, a flight into the azure afternoon, a sunset dropping of eggs on the shining surface of the river.

When the atmosphere lightens, what we call a rising glass, the nymphs hatch on the surface of the stream; trout rise, too, from their heaviness, for fish with their swim-bladders are most sensitive to air pressures.

In close thundery air, which affects you and me, trout lie torpid, as though suffering, on the bed of a river. When the air clears, up rise the nymphs of Olive Dun or Pale Watery, and whether you are a fisherman or not, you will be sharing the general lifting of the spirit, for the pressures upon the body always affect the mind.

And larks arise, the chaffinch sings in the hawthorn, turtle doves send their throbbing notes of love across the valley, the heart lifts with the clouds, and soon the vapours, metaphorical and physical, are gone. And the blue-stained air is without flaw.

Such was the morning when, without premeditation, I left my desk and walked outside and threw off my jacket and sat upon the grass. My shirt joined the jacket, and my vest by the gate through which I passed without any idea of where I was going or care for what I had been writing.

Over the hills and faraway, the sea, cerulean, fused with the sky. And gulls flying high, as though without aim, restless, turning about, stalling, flapping this way and that, as they criss-crossed the sky.

For this was the morning of the ants. For miles around, from every nest, the winged females were rising on the warm air. Trillions of ants. What made them all rise up and shine together, on those new wings? Scientists call it super-sensory perception: they receive the impulse, they fly up for love, borne into the blue on rising air. And those returning shed their wings, and start another colony underground.

And the green woodpecker will come to my field for them, uttering his yallery-greenery cry, *yaffle-yaffle-yaffle*, to announce his arrival. And drop his extraordinary little all-white cylinders, each one perfectly shaped, to dry in the sun. If you break one of the little cartridges with your fingers you will see that they are composed entirely of ant-skeletons bound by pure lime.

Now it is the turn of the rooks. They seem to have gone mad. They are twirling and cawing in the dome of the sky, rising on thermals and then hurtling down with wings closed and cawing and croaking for the joy of being alive.

I must explain that every rising column, or bubble of air as gliders call it, that bursts upwards causes a down-draught. In a black thunderhead charged with static electricity this can be very frightening if you are up in a glider.

I have a son, John, who, seeing a black bombard of a cloud approaching one summer day, got into the air and soon was being carried up in tight circles amidst the flash and crack of lightening until he was above the 27,000-foot contour, his wings icing up and he wearing only a tweed jacket and flannel trousers, and when he came down he had broken the British height record and all he could say to me was: 'I think I could have gone higher if the controls had not been frozen.'

Later he told me that the noise was terrifying, the up-draught was probably 100 m.p.h. and his fear was that if caught between the up and down air-rushes his wings might have been torn off. A boy of understatement from his earliest years.

Jackdaws were now joining the rooks in the upper air. They too were croaking deeply, they weren't after ants like the pale gulls, they were simply sporting. The sky had let down its hair, and its winged children were for the time being freed from economic necessity, and all its fears and anxieties. And my spirit went up with them.

The buzzards from Spreacombe Woods in the valley were now aloft. Five were sailing on broad cleaver-shaped wings serenely above the tumult. Nothing disturbed them. In ordinary workaday times rooks and crows would harry them, for the buzzard is slower in his sailing, circling flight than the dashing, cursing crows that snarl after the mewing hawk, with his nearly five-feet wingspread.

Afternoon came. I lay in the grass, free and uncaring. The moon rose up, I wandered home to my hut. And towards midnight I heard such a muttering and chortling that I went outside in pyjamas and walked through the dew to watch a prolonged ragged flight of rooks and jackdaws passing low over the beech spinney, flying from the east.

These birds had gone over Exmoor, simply for the hell of it, a great concourse of the Corvidae, and were now returning to their roosts – the rooks in Pickwell Wood just inland from the sea, and the daws to their holes and ledges down the cliffs of Baggy North Side.

And as I walked about the field, the moon cast my shadow before me, and I saw again that phenomenon, a sort of ring of light about the shadow of my head, which Richard Jefferies had mentioned in one of his books . . . Jefferies who also wrote, 'The hours when the soul is absorbed by beauty are the only hours when we truly live.'

4

ROBBIE: AN INNOCENT WHO BECAME FRIENDS WITH A HARE

While I was with a team 'filming' at my old home, Shallowford, by the Bray (which is the river of *Salar*) I was being watched by a small dog which had the look of a terrier about him, with the markings of a foxhound. The dog, which appeared to be young, stood still, just watching, outside the gate of the deer park. It belonged to the wife of Farmer Slee, a smallholder who lived in the lodge.

A fairly remote spot, Shallowford. One would think that a strange van arriving – of unusual shape – might at least cause a young dog to give one bark. But no. This animal showed a quiet and alert interest, while continuing to stand still.

When the filming, with my friend Kenneth Allsop, was over I asked Mrs. Slee about the dog.

'Robbie is quite old, over twelve years, but everyone says he looks like a puppy. He came to us because his old owner knocked him about a lot. You'll feel the bumps in his ribs, where they mended. Robbie still curls up in a corner, afraid of our boots. We're trying to find a home for him.'

Robbie rode back with me to my hilltop field. Whenever he saw a walking stick in anyone's hand he cringed away. It took a year to wean him from fear, before he could stretch out before the fire, and not turn an eye backward when I stepped over him to put on a log.

The only sign of his age was a suggestion of white hair about the muzzle, and his yellow teeth. If he saw another dog he made straight for it, even big dogs such as Alsatians. His tail vibrated, he showed no fear. They were soon friends racing over the grass, chasing and being chased.

Now I have been told in the past I am not a dog-lover. In theory yes, in practice no, said my friends. I was too self-absorbed, too withdrawn, always thinking about my books, often harassed, distraught. In early life I had found harmony from home by escaping into woods and fields and by streams, usually alone, blissfully being what my father called 'the wild-boy'.

That wonderful life-giving existence from which later was drawn, as water from a well, the essence for my earliest books, ended with a strange romantic merging into another world of the light of day displaced, of starlit nights not of owl-cry but of Plutonic gloom and terror; and yet of romance, as when I had discovered mystery in the woods of my boyhood. I would stand and stare on the battlefield greatly interested in this new world of iced shell-crater, frozen corpse, and flare of no man's land.

So while I was not a dog-lover, I had some sort of correlation with this Jack Russell-foxhound cross, with this extraordinary small dog which had been kicked and beaten and been made so afraid in its young years that it appeared not to have grown up, and with a sort of innocence which made it directly aware of the potential feelings of animate objects outside itself.

Was it too fanciful, I wondered, to think that Robbie, through his transcendental experiences, had become an innocent? For he seemed to know that we did not like to kill anything in the field, but live and let live. Thus he became friends with a wild hare which had its forme in the long grasses – left in the middle of the field as a nature reserve.

Once I saw Timid Wat the hare chasing Robbie through the hedge; then over the bank at the other end of the field came Timid Wat, chased back by Robbie. In the midst of the circling, doubling and reversing Timid Wat jumped sideways and Robbie turned and led Hare a dance across the next field. Of course Robbie knew that Timid Wat was a friend of mine. And also, he had beautiful manners.

And what a nose for scent! After one mid-August day when rain had fallen, the adjoining field of twenty acres, much grazed by sheep, by midnight was studded with mushrooms. Soon after dawn I was there with a basket and when I'd got enough for breakfast I hid from Robbie. He was huffing and snuffing down a mouse-hole in the field, upwind from me by a hundred yards. I remained flat on my back in the tall yellowing grasses and thistles, and never moved, except to raise my head slightly so that I could watch him.

When he realised that I was gone, he stood in his usual watching stillness, staring north. After a minute or so, he changed his stance to stare west, whence the wind was blowing. Then he stared south. And finally east, while I held myself unblinking. Then he trotted north to the thorn-grown bank, climbed up its slope and disappeared into the next field.

I lay in the grass, enjoying the early morning sunshine. Always my idea of bliss has been to lie on my back in the sun, close eyes, and float in spirit into a thoughtless realm. I lay there, hidden in the sere grasses of late summer, among the thistle cardoons soon to break into floss and each seed to float away under its parachute, while flocks of goldfinches twittered as they feasted.

I became a little anxious about Robbie. He was away a long time; then turning my head slightly I saw him sitting a yard away, looking at me. His foxhound blood had told him what to do: to make a circular cast and work up across the wind until he got my scent, and then follow it up wind.

They say a dog's age, comparable with a man's, is in the ratio of seven years to one. So Robbie was 98 years old, still young and fully aware, sensitive, never putting a foot wrong, as delicate as a roe-deer.

One day I saw signs of Robbie's unease. The vet said it was incurable: that it would grow worse, he would suffer; there were other considerations. He should be put down. A hard duty fell upon me.

For one whole morning I stood near him in a field, and when he had dug hard at a mouse-hole and his snout was well down and Robbie was blowing down it, *wuff* as though to drive the field mouse into the open, his eyes closed against the dust, I fired. He never saw me, he never knew he was hit, he lay quietly on his side, as though to sleep.

And today he still sleeps, under the pines along the eastern edge of the field, and a rhododendron grows from his grave.

5

NOW THE SUMMER SLIPS AWAY AND THE SUN GOES DOWN

AFTER toiling up the steep and sunken lane, almost enclosed by brambles and over-arching trees, I come to the sky-line and, suddenly, all is changed. There, far away and below, lie the Burrows, an area of sand-hills beside a sea-coast spreading away to the distant estuary of the Two Rivers, marked by the slim white tower of the lighthouse.

And the sea lies under an autumn sun to the horizon's curve. West of Hercules Promontory, as the Romans called the long rocky coastline of Hartland, lies the Atlantic, open to far Labrador. Drink in the sea-wind, absorb the azure of ocean fused with the sky. And turning to the south again, greet the hills of Dartmoor, a darker blue rising 40 miles away as the falcon glides.

In my young days I walked from this north coast of Devon to Dartmoor, and beyond to the Channel and round the coast to Sidmouth and thence to the Severn Sea and by way of footpaths above the red cliffs of Somerset back to this old-time haunt of mine, spread out below, the Burrows.

How still it is, how lonely on this hill. A wood lark sings somewhere on the stone wall. Those notes, they have a dying fall, as though for summer's requiem. All is so still.

The Burrows, wind-carved and wind-wrecked by the south-westerly gales, despite the hold of deep-rooted marram grass . . . The winter winds will soon be raving over the seashore, those level sands now smoothed by the lapsing tide.

East of the Burrows lie the Pans. Here on a soil holding brackish water grows the first vegetation of the land proper. Worthless to the farmer, the Pans remain in their primeval state. Here one sees many wild flowers, mosses, rushes, and dwarf willows – every kind of wild flower known to grow in England is to be found either on the Pans or the Burrows. There is the rare adder's-tongue fern; the club-headed rush which grows only in one other place in Britain. And the Great Sea Stock.

Beyond the Pans, a glint and gleam of the dykes, which carry fresh water from the hill-springs for cattle to drink as they graze rich grass which fattens them; a soil now deep, it is alluvial, silt accumulated during past millenia by the Two Rivers which begin as threads of water on the Great Kneeset, part of that blue hump along the southern horizon.

Taw and Torridge flow, each through its own valley and meet again in the estuary, by that white stalk of the lighthouse, which is my destination today; I, now free of the constrictions of the writing desk, once again ready to be instructed how to live by 'the great earth-smitten dandelion of the sun' of youth; I am in the company of Brother Wave and Sister Air.

So to the footpath down the hill, to the Burrows, that place of magic, of freedom, of restoration from the world which is too much with us.

The Burrows are in danger from that world. During the Hitlerian war tanks and flame-throwers and later amphibian craft exercised here. The Americans practised landings under live shell and curving red tracer. They built a road across this haunt of marsh harrier and wild geese in winter.

Once a Greenland falcon came south in a blizzard howling its way from the North Star. With the falcon came Bubu the great horned owl, birds with staring eyes, having seen the Aurora Borealis, Dawn of the Winter God, and their plumage had the hues of sleet and fog. Both, alas, to be seen later in the local taxidermist's window, for our arctic visitors were knocked over or trapped by some sportsman surviving from the Victorian age of shoot-and-stuff.

That was over forty years ago, in 1926, and you may read of that winter in a little local book called *Tarka the Otter*.

Yes, the Americans built this road, of hard core, almost to the lighthouse and the pebbled watery shore of the estuary. Now there is talk of a right-of-way, for the road has been built over twenty years. Gates have been put up by the owner – for the Burrows are private property – anyone may walk there, but what about cars? Will the Burrows become another Blackpool? But away with all corroding thoughts, do not heed the milk bottles and the yellowing scraps of August's newspapers.

My feet purr in the hot loose sand of the dunes and I fancy that I can hear the inaudible – or is it real? – music of this magic place. The sand is almost white under a bleaching sun which has however in its rays just a little of the melancholy of autumn.

I am alone in a hollow where four plants of the Great Sea Stock grew when I was here last, in June. And there was a Sea Holly, whose spiny leaves are as formidable to hand or naked foot as they are beautiful. Glaucous may be the word to describe their hue. If it is a wrong word I do not care, do not bother me with words while the still and hanging air is ringing with that strange remote music.

Is Ariel come again? Those eyes of sapphire, the gentle lips of beauty entranced, the whisper of the name Prospero. Did I dream it once? All life is a dream. The music descends and rises within an octave, falling and rising about the azure. Just here, beside me, where the prints of feet lead to the wind's oblivion.

On a calm day such as this the Atlantic pulse is turned to gentleness. A wave rises thin and creams over at its leading edge and falls tinkling with sun-drops on my face and back. I have miles of sand to myself and my clothes lie on the shore scattered, and only the ring-plovers and shore-larks see me in the water.

> Sabrina fair,
> Listen where thou art sitting
> Under the glassie, cool, translucent wave.
> In twisted braids of lilies knitting
> The loose train of thy amber-dropping hair.
> Listen for dear honour's sake,
> Goddess of the silver lake,
> Listen and save – *

Someone in the summer, which is gliding away, seems to have wrenched out the Great Sea Stocks, which grew there in June. Their roots are strong and thick, like flexible canes. Some innocent child, maybe: but the seeds have dropped, there will be flowers here next June.

Now the sun has gone down below the rim of the ocean, night is coming to the earth. I lie under the streaming light of the western stars, the driftwood fire is wan with dying embers. One last look around from the crest of the tallest sand hill above the Valley of the Winds. Those flashings along the rim of ocean are from the

[* from *Comus* (1637), by John Milton]

lighthouse towers of Lundy and Hartland. They will be there on the way back.

Evening Standard, 16-20 November, 1964